IF GOD IS IN CONTROL, THEN WHY…?

Trusting a Just God in an Unjust World

BY

CRAIG HILL

FAMILY FOUNDATIONS INTERNATIONAL
LITTLETON, COLORADO
WWW.FAMILYFOUNDATIONS.COM

Family Foundations International
P.O. Box 320
Littleton, Colorado 80160

Printed in the United States of America

All Scripture quotations are taken from The New King James Bible unless otherwise noted: *The New King James Bible*, Thomas Nelson Publishers, 1982; *The New American Standard Bible*, (NASB), The Lockman Foundation, 1960, 1962, 1963, 1968, 1971, 1973, 1975

The characters in many of the examples cited in this book are real life people whom the author has known. For their privacy, however, some names and some of the insignificant details have been altered. Alternatively, some incidents described are not sequential events, but are composites of several incidents; nevertheless, they reflect very real situations.

DEDICATION
TO ROSS DUDLEY

Just as the editing of this book was being completed, my good friend and ministry co-laborer, Ross Dudley, suffered a massive heart attack and passed away. During the last couple of years, I spent many hours bouncing ideas off of Ross, and discussing the practical outworking in real life of the principles described in this book. Because he believed and lived these principles, I dedicate the book to Ross in memory of his life and ministry on earth. Ross was a very kind and generous man who naturally lived out the qualities of a godly father and spiritual leader listed in Titus 1:6-9.

A couple of weeks before he passed away, Ross celebrated his fiftieth birthday. For that occasion, I wrote a letter, part of which I would like to quote here:

> "Happy Fiftieth Birthday, Ross! You are an incredible blessing to Jan and me. We count it such a privilege to get to work with you in the ministry and to count you as our friend. Some of the qualities I really appreciate about you are that you are totally loyal, reliable, trustworthy, (clean, reverent, friendly, cheerful, helpful, courteous, kind and other such Boy Scout qualities). The amazing thing is that, all kidding aside, these qualities really are

true of you. You don't try to exemplify these characteristics. They just are who you are."

Thanks Ross, for having lived your life in such a way as to be an example to others, and to make us proud to have known you.

ACKNOWLEDGEMENTS

I want to give special thanks to the following, who helped in the review, editing and typesetting of this book:

My wife and best friend, Jan

Mackenzie Bragg (FFI staff, Colorado)

Pastor Neil Campbell, Calgary, Alberta, Canada

Arabelle Hinchliff (FFI staff, Colorado)

Crystal McClung, Colorado Springs, Colorado

Pastor Bruce Mulberry, Pottstown, Pennsylvania

And for the graphics design of the book cover:
Jason Dudley (FFI staff, Colorado)

Additional Resources are listed at the end of each chapter. Unless noted, resources are by Craig Hill. Resources are available through Family Foundations International. To locate an FFI office near you, please visit our website at www.familyfoundations.com.

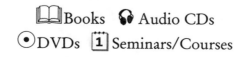

Books Audio CDs
DVDs Seminars/Courses

CONTENTS

INTRODUCTION

In this book, we will look into the function and operation of evil and injustice on the earth, and how we are to interpret experiences filled with such in our own lives. As we look at this issue of how to interpret life's circumstances, or really any other issue, I find that truth is most often like a road. There is always a ditch on either side of the road, and the enemy doesn't care into which ditch you fall. The trick is to keep on the road without driving off into either ditch. Of course, as soon as we see one ditch, the tendency is to attempt to move as far away from that ditch as possible (thesis – antithesis). However, in attempting to avoid the ditch we now see, I think that we frequently jump all the way across the road right into the other ditch, not realizing that we have done so. All we know is that we will never again be accused of being in that first ditch, because we are far away from it.

I have found in my experience that God's purpose in all of life's experiences is to draw us into relationship with Him. He loves us and desires intimate relationship. Consequently, all of life was designed to lead us into intimate relationship with God. I believe that His desire is to partner with you and me to accomplish His Kingdom purpose and to expand His

Kingdom rule and reign throughout the whole earth. However, it seems that we are constantly tempted in life to abandon relationship and partnership with God. We easily decide that life is either all about God, or that life is all about me. These are two ditches on either side of the road.

Ditch #1: God is in Control

Let me help define each of these ditches a little more so that perhaps we can avoid falling in either one of them. One ditch focuses on God's responsibility on earth. A man who interprets life's circumstances from this ditch does not understand or acknowledge his responsibility to partner with God as His Kingdom representative on earth. When things are not going well, he simply says, "Well, God is in control. I'll just trust Him and it will all work out in the end." In doing so, he is actually abdicating his authority and responsibility to partner with God. Rather than pressing in to seek God's face, he is in reality abandoning his relationship with God and hoping that God will act independent of him.

Ditch #2: Man is in Control

On the other hand, some people in the opposite ditch focus on their authority and responsibility before God. A man who interprets life from this ditch believes that he has discovered principles and keys to particular aspects of life. He then believes that if he will just apply these principles (independently of God), life will work fine. Again, in doing so this he breaks partnership with God and results in his becoming prideful, independent and self-reliant, thus trying to use God's Word and God's principles without God. When things don't go well, he then says, "I am really being attacked by the devil. However, I will persist and persevere because I know that the Word always works, and in the end, we win." Just like the man in the opposite ditch, rather than pressing in to seek God's face, this man is also abandoning relationship with God and believing that God's Word will produce the desired fruit independent of relationship.

Either of these ditches, of course, sets one up for defeat and failure. God has established the world in such a way that life requires us to walk in partnership and relationship with Him. One of the key scripture verses that the LORD has given us in our ministry is a description of how Jesus Himself functioned in relationship with His Father while He walked on earth. Even Jesus could not simply take true

> God has established the world in such a way that life requires us to walk in partnership and relationship with Him.

principles or keys to life and implement them independent of His relationship with His Father. On the other hand, Jesus also realized that being in relationship with the Father meant that He had a responsibility to see what the Father was doing, and then act as His representative. Thus Jesus said regarding His function on earth:

> *Most assuredly I say to you, the Son can do nothing of Himself, but what He sees the Father do; for whatever He does, the Son also does in like manner.* (John 5:19)

Thus we see that both of the two ditches on either side of the road lead us to live a life that is independent of intimate and vital relationship with Jesus Christ. Although either ditch is equally dangerous, I have chosen in this book to focus primarily on the problems associated with interpreting life's circumstances from the first ditch I described above; that of seeing life as all God's responsibility. However, in this introduction I wanted to initially point out the ditch on the other side of the road. This may help us not to jump all the way over into the other ditch in an attempt to avoid this first ditch. So as you read the book, please keep in mind that there is indeed a ditch on either side of the road. As you work this through in your own life experience, please endeavor to remain upon the road in relationship with the One Who loves you and for the sake of eternal relationship with you, was willing to give up His life and die.

chapter 1
Is God In Control?

God is in control! Many times we hear people use this phrase, intending to express a trust in God rather than a trust in circumstances or in self. But what does this cliché really mean? Does it mean that everything that happens on the earth is God's idea and functions according to His plan? Even as I write this book, just a few days ago a troubled young man shot and killed two young missionaries on a Youth With a Mission base in our city, and then proceeded a few hours later to shoot and kill two young teenage women and himself at New Life Church in Colorado Springs. Was this God's plan? Did He desire and intend for these five young people to be killed at this time? If so, then was the young shooter led by God to kill these people? If not, then where was God? If He is in control, then why did He allow this to happen? If He is not in control, is life on planet earth out of control? How do we answer such questions? If God is in control, and yet evil and injustice are perpetrated against us anyway, how then are we supposed to respond?

I was forced to question the cliché, "God is in control" many years ago when I first began to attempt to share the Gospel of Jesus Christ with people who had no personal relationship with God. At a very early point in the conversation, each person with whom I began to share would raise the question of evil and injustice in the world. The question would go something like the following: "If your God is so loving and so powerful, then why did _____ happen?" Each person would have a different scenario of evil or injustice, such as the death of an innocent child, the murder or untimely death of a parent or relative, a crippling or debilitating disease afflicting a loved one, etc. The question always was, "If God is in control, as you say, then why did He let this happen?" The conclusion of many such people was that if God were truly in control, but yet allowed such blatant evil and injustice to prevail as that person had experienced or observed, then He could not be trusted. This made it difficult to convince many unbelievers to entrust their lives to Jesus Christ.

As I continued to ponder this question and talk with other believers, I soon came to realize that while many unbelievers will voice this question, most believers also struggle with the same question, but simply don't articulate it. Many times believers attempt to comfort each other with scriptural or cultural clichés such as, "Well, you know, God's ways are not our ways, and His thoughts are not our thoughts," or, "We don't understand everything. Some things we'll just have to wait until we get to heaven to ask," or "God moves in strange and mysterious ways." If the truth were known, many believers have a huge dichotomy between their head and their heart. I have found that many people who have personally experienced great injustice or evil will state with their mouths that God is good, but in their heart of hearts they don't believe it.

In past years there has been a phrase that was spoken out in many churches promoting the goodness of God. A leader would shout from the front of the congregation, "God is good." The congregation would then respond, "All the time." The leader would then exclaim, "And all the time." The people would then respond, "God is good." This chant would then go back and forth several times, "God is good; all the time. And all the time; God is good." I believe that the reason this became quite popular is because so many people deep in their hearts do not believe that God is good. If God is truly in control, then the obvious question in the hearts of men on planet earth is, "Why is there such a prevalence of evil and injustice? Why doesn't God just stop the evil and injustice? Why does He allow it?" Some of the logical answers to these questions may be as follows. Evil and injustice seem to prevail on the earth because:

- God really is not good. He, Himself, is evil and wants the earth to be this way.

- God is busy and in general doesn't care. He certainly doesn't concern Himself with my little puny problem of evil or injustice.

- God created the world long ago, set everything in motion, and is no longer involved and doesn't realize how bad it really is.

- God is good and He does care, but He is powerless to really change things.

- God is good and He does care, but His plans of how to deal with evil are not very wise and just don't work in reality.

- God is good, but evil is a part of his discipline and training process. He initiates, orchestrates, and utilizes injustice and evil to build character and teach us something. Therefore, from God's perspective, evil is not really bad, but is actually good from a long-term perspective.

Sovereignty Versus Control

Through the years as I have pondered this question, none of the answers above have really set right with me. So I began to question the thesis upon which each of the above conclusions is based. These are all predicated upon the thesis that God is in control. What if God were not in control? At least not in the classical sense that many people have been taught. Now before you put the book down and quit reading right here, let me quickly say that while I do not believe that God is in control, I do believe that God is sovereign. This distinction has greatly helped me to understand God's character and interpret life's circumstances.

I have discovered that there is a great difference between sovereignty and control. It may seem that this is just a subtle semantic difference. However, what we are actually talking about here is the way in which God governs men and women upon the earth. Although the concepts conveyed by the words *control* and *sovereignty* may seem similar, the systems of government pertaining to each word are very different. Let's look at these two different systems of government.

Government by exercising Control: Control implies an absolute dominion over that which is governed. Possessing supreme power and utilizing it in such a way as to ensure a particular outcome. Control is the process of governing through a manipulative power that forces people and circumstances to conform to the will of the one in control. Control eliminates the will or choices of others and only recognizes one will; that of the one who exercises control.

OR Government by exercising Sovereign Authority: Sovereign Authority implies an absolute ownership of that which is governed. It is the state of being the highest authority, with submission to no higher authority. Possessing supreme power and utilizing it by subjecting power to legitimate delegated authority. Sovereignty recognizes the will and choices of all people. It therefore governs through delegated authority, offering choices with corresponding applied consequences.

Let me briefly also provide two other definitions that may be helpful in understanding these concepts:

Power: The force necessary to accomplish the desired purpose.

Authority: The right to govern and exercise power.

Let's clarify by example the difference between power and authority. A car may be sitting at an intersection waiting for the stoplight to turn green. If the car is full of fuel, and the engine is functioning properly, then the driver has the power to progress through the intersection. However, if the stoplight is red, then the driver, while having the power, lacks the authority to progress. On the other hand, if the fuel tank in the car is empty and the motor has died, then when the light turns green, the driver now has the authority to progress through the intersection, but lacks the power.

By these above definitions, it became very clear to me that God is not a controller and does not govern the earth by control. He has absolute power, but does not use His power to force His will to be accomplished. Control is something you exercise over equipment, money, or things, but not over people. You control your car. You don't recognize the will of your car and offer it the choice to turn right or turn left. NO! You simply use your power to manipulate the steering wheel and force the car to accomplish your will. However, this is not how God has called us to treat people.

In governing people, we are called to use God's system of exercising authority, rather than control. Control uses manipulative power to force others to do my will. Control dictates the outcome regardless of the choices of people. The exercise of authority, on the other hand, motivates others to make wise choices by acknowledging the will of others and by offering them choices with appropriate corresponding applied consequences.

So if God were truly in control, there would be no question as to the outcome of every circumstance and event on earth. The observed outcome of every event would ultimately have to be considered to be the will of God. Thus, if we observe the function of evil or injustice, and if God is in control, we would have to consider the observed evil to be the will of God. However, our own hearts and consciences by nature tell us otherwise. When we hear of an evil man who breaks into a home, plunders the goods, rapes a young daughter, and murders the father and mother in front of the daughter and her younger brothers and sisters, our own hearts tell us that this was not God's will and that there is no way that God planned this, or stood by and "allowed" this because He was "in control."

In reality, God certainly has the knowledge, wisdom, and power to eliminate all evil and injustice on the earth. So if God were truly in control, there would be no drug dealers on earth. There would be no murderers or rapists on the earth. There would be no sexual predators or child molesters on the earth. He certainly has the power and wisdom to stop all sin. So if God were truly in control, there would be no sin on the earth, and therefore, in reality, no sinners on the earth. This would also mean that there would be no people on the earth. However, we observe that we still do have both people and sin on the earth. These observations lead me to the conclusion that God is not in control!

As you may have already concluded yourself, there is a missing piece to this puzzle that we have not yet talked about. If God is not in control, then two other questions immediately come to mind: "What prevents God from controlling evil and stopping it?" and "Do Satan, demons, and wicked people then have free reign on the earth to do whatever they will?" The answer is, "NO!" There is a mitigating force that works in conjunction with God's power and wisdom that limits the spread of sin and evil on the earth. We will look into a more complete discussion of the answer to these two questions in chapters three and four.

Examples of God's Sovereign Authority

What then does it mean that God is not in control, but that He does exercise sovereign authority? I believe this means that God has supreme power to do anything He chooses, but has voluntarily limited Himself to work through delegated authority. God's sovereignty empowers Him to invade human life on earth to affect circumstances and human experience without violating the free will given to men.

Whatever the Lord pleases, He does, in heaven and in earth, in the seas, and in all the deep places. Psalm 135:6

So we see that the scripture declares that God is not limited in His power to do whatever He pleases in heaven or on earth. Many of us have heard of, and perhaps personally experienced, God's sovereign, supernatural intervention in our lives. The fact that God is not in control does not mean that He is not involved or cannot intervene in our lives and human experience. I would like, at this point, to share with you several examples of God's sovereign intervention in my life and in the lives of others I have known.

God Flew the Airplane

My father related to me an experience that occurred during World War II in the life of a friend of his. This friend, Bobby (not his real name), was a P-47 fighter pilot in the European theater of war. One day in air combat with the Germans over France, Bobby's plane was severely shot up and damaged. He escaped from the Luftwaffe by entering a cloud. As he came out the other side of the cloud, there were no more enemy planes in sight, but unfortunately Bobby discovered that his P-47 had sustained significant damage to the airframe. The damage was such that he found he had no pitch, roll or yaw control.

Bobby reported that he could move the control stick full range from side to side and forward and aft with no affect whatsoever on the airplane. The only control he had was to increase or retard the throttle. Recognizing his life-threatening situation, Bobby quickly cried out to God in the name of the Lord Jesus Christ for help to spare his life and get him safely to the ground. Bobby then reported that something very supernatural began to happen. Expecting to have to bail out over enemy territory, Bobby found instead his P-47 had righted itself into a level flight position headed to the west toward England. Not knowing what else to do, Bobby let go of all the airplane controls and continued to pray, no longer really being a pilot, but rather just a passenger in his P-47, which seemed to be remaining level and on a course for England all by itself.

After some time, Bobby's airplane flew out over the channel and soon he saw the cliffs of Dover disappear under the nose of his airplane. He thought, "Now if I crash or must bail out, at least I will not be in hostile territory, behind enemy lines." Amazingly, a short time later, Bobby saw his home airbase come into view and his P-47 was perfectly lined up with the runway several miles ahead. Since he did have control over the power, Bobby retarded the throttle, manually lowered the landing gear, and used power to control his rate of descent toward the runway. With no control over his pitch, roll, or yaw, the airplane supernaturally continued on a straight course for the runway at his home airbase, and Bobby simply continued to control his rate of descent by reducing the throttle. As the airplane touched down safely on the runway, Bobby dedicated the rest of his life to serve Jesus Christ and thanked God for His supernatural, sovereign intervention to fly the airplane all the way back to England with no pilot control available.

God Paid the Bills

In the late 1960s my father, Gilman Hill, was struggling financially to recover from a prior business disaster. As a petroleum geologist, he had studied a particular geologic basin full of natural gas, in which many gas wells had been drilled by several major companies. However, these companies had not properly understood that the reservoir rock containing the gas was so impermeable that although these rocks contained a huge volume of gas, it would take decades to recover it at the present flow rates.

Dad thought that he had discovered a potential solution for producing the gas more rapidly and approached several of these companies with his proposal. However, he found that not only were these companies not interested, but they were also so discouraged that they just wanted to eliminate the leases in the basin that they held and get the failed project off of their books. They no longer wanted to have to report this failed project to their superiors and stockholders.

Consequently, several of these companies offered Dad the "opportunity" to take title to their leases in this basin if he would simply agree to pay the annual rental feel to the U.S. government of $1 per acre. Dad agreed to do so, believing that these leases would be productive at some time in the future. However, the next month after he took assignment of the first group of leases, he received a bill from the government for over $30,000. He had no money with which to pay this bill, so he assumed that he would probably have to forfeit the leases. However, a few days before the bill was due, another small company called Dad asking if they could purchase a few sections of the leases he owned at a price sufficient to pay the lease rentals that month, plus enough to purchase the food to feed his family.

The next month, he had another amount due on lease rentals. The companies who were assigning the leases to him, of course, were motivated to get rid of their leases shortly before the next year's rental payments were due. Dad had no money with which to pay the rentals. Again, shortly before the end of the month, someone called him wanting to buy some equipment they could salvage located on his leases. The amount offered was exactly the amount due for lease rentals that month plus food for his family. Again, Dad was surprised and thought that he was really lucky.

To make a long story shorter, this same scenario continued month after month for over a year. After several months, Dad began to realize that this was not just luck, but rather that God was sovereignly intervening in his life for a purpose. At that point, he began to acknowledge God's hand in this matter and thank Him for it. This began an incredible journey in my father's life with the Lord, which led him to drill an exploratory well in search of oil in Israel, and have opportunity to meet with and pray for then PLO Chairman, Yasser Arafat and other key Israeli and Palestinian leaders. Many of these subsequent ventures were funded with finances generated from the production of the gas resources located on those original leases given to my dad and sovereignly paid for by God's supernatural intervention in his life.

God Spared My Life (Several Times)

It seems that there was a tremendous spiritual battle for my life during the year I was sixteen years old. I wasn't aware of it then, but I think that if I would have been able to see into the unseen spirit realm at that time, the scenario may have looked like something out of a Frank Peretti novel. I was almost killed three times that year.

During my teenage years, I had a great interest in air sports. I had learned to fly gliders, aerobatic airplanes, hot air balloons, and became a skydiving instructor. One summer morning, I was flying a hot air balloon over the south end of our city. As it had become a little late in the morning, the sun had already begun to create thermal up and down drafts. In addition, the wind had virtually died altogether.

Unfortunately, this had happened while my balloon had drifted right over the top of some high-tension power lines. I went up and down several thousand feet attempting to find a wind that would blow me off of the power lines, but it seemed that any wind that existed was only blowing me directly parallel to the power lines, not off to the side of them.

I had now been flying for a couple of hours and was running low on propane fuel. I had attempted to work my way off to the side of the power lines several times. Each time I began to try to descend, a thermal downdraft would grab me and begin to plummet me toward the earth too close to the power lines and faster than I wanted to go. I would then attempt to check the descent rate by blasting hot air into the balloon. I would inevitably over-blast and ascend back up again.

I had repeated this scenario several times already and was now running out of fuel. I thought, "If I don't hurry up and land, I'm going to run out of fuel and then I'll have no choice where or when I come down." I managed to work the balloon slightly off to the side of the power lines again and began my descent. Suddenly, a thermal downdraft grabbed the balloon, rotated it right over the top of the power lines, and began to plummet me toward the lines. I immediately began to blast hot air back up into the balloon, but it soon became evident to me that I would not be able to put enough heat into the balloon fast enough to overcome the downward momentum. (The hot air balloon burners in those days only supplied about ¼ of the hot air that the burners do in more modern balloons.)

As the balloon and basket headed toward the power lines, I realized that in about twelve seconds, one of two things would happen. When the balloon basket hit the power lines,

16

either the propane tanks would explode, or I would be electrocuted by the power running through the lines. Since there was nothing more I could naturally do, I began to cry out to God to save me as I descended toward the lines. In addition, I sat on the edge of the basket, thinking that maybe I would jump just before the basket hit the power lines. The fall would be about fifty feet, but I thought that maybe I would live.

As I was preparing to jump, only a few feet above the power lines, the thermal downdraft suddenly shifted the balloon and basket to the other side of the power lines. I climbed back into the basket just as the balloon basket missed the power lines by only a few feet. I pulled the red line unsealing the top of the balloon, allowing it to deflate on the ground.

Soon after safely reaching the ground, I realized, for the first time in my life that God was not just a religious concept, but that He was a real Person who actually knew me, heard me cry out to Him, and had intervened to save my life. I didn't know what to do with that information at that time. Unfortunately, it was another three years until I learned that it was possible to have a personal relationship and two-way conversation with God every day.

I would also like to share one other experience that occurred during the same year. Our family had a four wheel drive Ford Bronco that I liked to take up in our Colorado mountains on jeep trails. One particular weekend, I had taken the Bronco, by myself, on a trail up the west side of Mount Evans. The trail had taken me up to about 12,500 feet above sea level, nearing the 14,000-foot summit. I was climbing up a fairly steep hill on an open slope above timberline when I decided that the slope was steeper than I wished to navigate. So rather than back the Bronco down the mountain the way I had come, I decided to turn around and then head back down forwards.

As I turned the vehicle perpendicular to the fall line of the slope, the right rear wheel slipped downhill off of a small six-inch tall rock. This slip gave enough momentum to roll the entire vehicle, which was now facing sideways on the slope. The Bronco rolled ninety degrees onto its side and stopped, virtually suspended in the air. I was sitting in the left hand driver's seat suspended on the uphill side of the vehicle looking down over a thousand feet, wondering why the vehicle was not rolling. I sat motionless, afraid that if I moved, I might cause the Bronco to roll. As I surveyed the situation, I noticed that the right (downhill) shoulder of the vehicle, just ahead of the passenger door, was pinned against a large pinnacle-like rock. The vehicle was perfectly balanced against this rock at a point apparently very near the center of gravity, preventing the Bronco from slipping around the rock and plummeting down the mountainside.

I shut off the engine, left the vehicle in gear, set the parking brake, and very carefully climbed out of the Bronco. It was over a ten-mile walk back down the mountain trail to a road where I could find a ride back to town. (We didn't have cell phones yet in those days.) The next weekend, some members of the Colorado 4-wheel drive club drove back up to that location and used their winches and several vehicles to rescue the Bronco. Several of the members who went to rescue the vehicle commented that it was a miracle that I had not rolled down the entire slope, and that there had "happened to be" a large pinnacle rock at just the exact place to catch the shoulder of the Bronco as it started to roll. Again, I saw the sovereign hand of God at work to save my life. I had a couple of other experiences with airplanes and parachutes that same year, in which I saw God sovereignly move on my behalf.

I have shared these stories with you to illustrate the point that God is definitely involved in the lives of men and women on planet earth in a sovereign way. In each of the above instances, we see God intervening in the lives of people on earth to accomplish a specific purpose in their lives. However, in none of these instances did God ever force any person or violate their will.

Reflection

1. God is sovereign, but He is not in control.

2. God governs men by offering choices with consequences. He does not force, manipulate or control people.

3. God does sovereignly invade our lives to accomplish His purposes.

4. What experiences of God's supernatural intervention have you had in your life?

chapter 2
GOD'S WILL AND
GOVERNANCE

As I began to ponder the implications of the thought that maybe God is sovereign, but not in control, another question came to my mind. If God is not in control, is it possible then for men on earth to thwart or stop the will of God? How does God administrate His will on earth? This led me to do a word study in the Bible on the word used for "will" as it pertains to God.

I remembered hearing my friend, Earl Pitts, who had co-authored with me the book, *Wealth, Riches & Money*[1], talk about two different Greek words in the Bible translated in English as the word "will." As I studied these words that the Holy Spirit chose to use in the Bible, it seemed to me that they really were describing two different aspects of the will of God. Without dividing these two aspects for clarification,

---

[1] Hill, Craig and Pitts, Earl. *Wealth, Riches & Money.* Littleton: Family Foundations International, 2001

it is almost impossible to answer some questions regarding the will of God.

WAS IT THE WILL OF GOD FOR JUDAS TO BETRAY JESUS?

For example, one might ask, "Was it the will of God for Judas to betray Jesus?" If you were a biblical counselor at that time and Judas came to you for counsel, indicating that he was thinking of selling Jesus out to the Pharisees, would you advise him to do so, or not to do so? We know from Scripture that it was the will of God for Messiah to be betrayed and to die on the cross. So if you counseled Judas to betray Him would you not be supporting the will of God? On the other hand, how could you, with a clear conscience, advise anyone to betray Jesus and participate in killing an innocent man? So what is the answer? I have found that this question can only be answered by understanding these two concepts of the will of God.

The two Greek words that somewhat correlate with these two concepts of the will of God are transliterated in English as *Boulema* and *Thelema*. Both of these words are translated in our English Bibles many times as the word "will." Their meanings are not one hundred percent consistent in every scriptural use, but there is a clear and evident distinction between two different concepts conveyed by the one English word "will." These two distinct concepts I will term as the "unalterable purpose" will of God, and the "desire" will of God. Let me give more definition to the way in which I will use these concepts in this book.

Unalterable purpose: God's sovereign determination of events. His absolute choice of what will come to pass; God's sovereign **purpose**, His determined resolve.

Desire: An expression of God's **desire**, intent and want for life on planet earth; that expression which is consistent with His nature and character.

By these definitions, unalterable purpose is that intentional action which God will sovereignly implement and no man can stop. Examples of the **"unalterable purpose"** will of God would be some of the following:

- Jesus will be betrayed and die on the cross for the sin of all humanity.
- God will restore the land of Israel physically to the Hebrew people.
- The antichrist will rise up and defile the temple in Jerusalem.
- Jesus Christ will return physically to the earth and will rule and reign here for one thousand years.

These things will happen and no one will stop them.

Examples of the **"desire"** will of God would be some of the following:

- It is God's will to heal sick people.
- It is God's will for a man to love his wife and not to physically abuse her.
- It is God's will for fathers to love their children and not to sexually violate them.
- It is God's will that men who own businesses treat their customers fairly and with integrity, not lying to or cheating them.

These are God's desires consistent with His nature and character, but we observe that these things do not always happen as God wills.

So if we return to the question of whether it was God's will for Judas to betray Jesus, I think that we would now conclude:

- unalterable purpose – yes
- desire – no

Now, I would always counsel the "desire" will of God; that which is in accordance with His desire, character, and nature. I am convinced that God would have known, and Satan would have found someone else to betray Jesus, had I succeeded in convincing Judas not to do so. However, Judas still had a choice, and God knew what that choice would be even though it was the" unalterable purpose" will of God that Jesus be betrayed.

Let me now give you some scriptural examples of the usage of both "unalterable purpose" will and "desire" will. First are some examples of the "desire" will:

Your kingdom come. Your <u>will</u> be done on earth as it is in heaven. (Matthew 6:10)

But go and learn what this means, "I <u>desire</u> (will) mercy and not sacrifice." For I did not come to call the righteous, but sinners, to repentance. (Matthew 9:13)

Not everyone who says to Me, 'Lord, Lord,' shall enter the kingdom of heaven, but he who does the <u>will</u> of My Father in heaven. (Matthew 7:21)

In each of these above cases, we see that the word "will" is used to describe the desire and intention of God. Jesus told us to pray in Matthew 6 for the will of God to be done on earth. We don't have to pray for the unalterable purpose of

24

God to be done. It will be done, and no one will stop it. We do, however, need to pray for the intention and desire of God to be done. Let's now look at a couple of examples of the "unalterable purpose" will of God in scripture.

For men indeed swear by the greater, and an oath, for confirmation is for them an end of all dispute. Thus God, determining (willing) to show more abundantly to the heirs of promise the immutability of His counsel (will), confirmed it by an oath, that by two immutable things, in which it is impossible for God to lie, we might have strong consolation, who have fled for refuge to lay hold of the hope set before us. (Hebrews 6:16-18)

The Lord is not slack concerning His promise, as some count slackness, but is longsuffering toward us, not willing that any should perish but that all should come to repentance. (2 Peter 3:9)

The obvious point in the passage above is that if it were the unalterable purpose of God that none should perish, then none would perish! However, we observe that many do perish. Therefore, again we can see that it is the desire and intent of God that none should perish. He doesn't want any to perish. However, it is not His will (unalterable purpose) that none should perish. Let's now look at a scriptural example in which both Greek words and distinct concepts for will are used in the same verse.

And He was withdrawn from them about a stone's throw, and He knelt down and prayed, saying, 'Father, if it is Your will (unalterable purpose)

25

take this cup away from Me; nevertheless not My will (desire), but Yours, be done. (Luke 22:41-42)

In this verse, we see Jesus using these two words for will in the way we have described. Using these words the way we have defined them, He is saying something like the following, "Father, if it would not disrupt your unalterable purpose, please change my circumstance and take this cup from me. However, I am here on the earth to accomplish your desire and pleasure, not My own. Therefore, I will not only submit to your unalterable purpose, but I will also submit to your desire and wishes, even at the expense of My own short-term comfort and desire."

Two Systems of Government

Earlier in chapter one, we talked about the fact that God governs people on earth through the sovereign exercise of authority, but not through control. These are really two entirely different ways of governing. Satan is a controller and seeks to govern people through force, threats, and control. I have observed that various people on earth utilize either God's system of the exercise of authority, or Satan's system of control, within the context of human organizations such as families, companies, or nations. Some countries govern their citizens through offering choices with applied consequences, while other countries govern their citizens by force.

God has always governed men by the exercise of authority and not by control. Let me give you an example of God's dealings with His people Israel in Deuteronomy chapter 30.

See I have set before you today life and good, death and evil, in that I command you today to love the Lord your God, to walk in His ways, and to keep His commandments, His statutes, and His judgments, that you may live and multiply; and the Lord your God will bless you in the land which you go to possess.... I call heaven and earth as witnesses today against you, that I have set before you blessing and cursing; therefore choose life, that both you and your descendants may live. (Deuteronomy 30:15-16; 19)

In these scripture verses we see God imploring Israel to choose life and blessing. He does not force them or control them. When they partner with Him, He does supernatural events for them such as the Passover deliverance and parting the Red Sea. Here we see God command the people to walk in His ways and keep His statutes, but the choice remains theirs. He explains to them that they have a choice to experience either life or death, blessing or curse.

Regarding the New Covenant, we observe that God has never forced anyone to Jesus Christ. Rather, He offers people choices with consequences. In essence we see God saying to people, "You are separated from Me by your sin. Jesus Christ died in your place to make a way to connect you to Me in covenant by His blood sacrifice. You have a choice. You may continue to have your sin counted against you and remain separated from me for all eternity by rejecting the blood sacrifice of Jesus Christ. Or you may have your sin forgiven and enter into relationship with me and live eternally in My presence. I implore you to make the second choice and receive Jesus Christ. However, the choice is yours. I will not force you."

Then how does God respond to people who choose to retain accountability for their own sin and remain separated from God for eternity? Is he angry with them? Does He yell and scream at them? No! He weeps for them because He loves them.

Let's now look at how these two systems of government function within a family. Many families actually govern their family members utilizing Satan's system of control, rather than God's system of the exercise of authority. Most parents tend to govern their children utilizing the same system in which they were raised. Let's contrast the system of control with the system of the exercise of authority. What does the system of control look like?

Firstly, in such a family there is a rule maker, and by definition the rule maker is always right. The rule maker is usually dad or mom, and his/her job is to control the behavior of everyone in the family. Therefore everyone must always be "right" and do everything "right." Of course, the rule maker decides what "right" is. If you make a mistake or something gets out of control, you are then shamed, ridiculed, and punished by the rule maker. The primary way the rule maker governs others in the family is to attempt to control them and force them to do what is "right."

Open This Door

One example comes to mind. Bill had a seventeen-year-old son, Matt, who was quite rebellious. Bill and Matt had not had a very good relationship for several years. Unfortunately, Bill had grown up under the system of control and had sought to govern his family in the same way. One evening Matt was in his room with the door locked. He decided to play very loudly a CD that his dad had forbidden to be in the house due to the lyrical content.

When Bill heard this music and the forbidden lyrics, he became quite upset and angry. When Bill went upstairs to Matt's room, he noticed some smoke billowing out from under Matt's door. Bill could tell that the smoke was not regular tobacco smoke. He rather suspected that it was marijuana smoke, although he didn't know exactly what marijuana smelled like.

Bill's anger now intensified as he knocked on the door and demanded that Matt open the door immediately and let him in.

"Matt, you open this door right now!" he yelled.

There was no response.

"Son, this is your father. I demand that you open the door this instant! I want to talk with you."

Still no response, but the music got louder.

By this time Bill was furious. He began pounding on the door with his fists, his face beet red, and veins popping out on his neck.

"Matt, you open this door immediately! If you don't you'll be grounded for a year!"

Matt, of course, never did respond. There was nothing Bill could do, so he eventually went back downstairs and decided that he would confront his son in the morning. The next morning, when Matt came down for breakfast, his father was waiting for him. The moment Matt appeared in the room, Bill began his tirade.

"What were you doing in the room last night? Was that marijuana smoke I smelled? Why didn't you open the door when I knocked and asked you to? No son of mine is going to act like that in my house. You #@*&% kid!"

As his father yelled at him, Matt just sat unresponsively at the table eating his bowl of cereal. After Bill finished yelling, he looked at Matt and queried, "So what do you have to say for yourself?"

"Whatever!" exclaimed Matt, as he walked out the door to head to school.

All of Matt's life, Bill had tried to control Matt's behavior. Now, at seventeen, Matt was too big to be physically controlled by Bill. Consequently, Bill was now at a loss as to how to control Matt. Over the next weekend, Bill attended a seminar with his wife in which he learned the difference between Satan's system of control and God's system of exercising authority. Bill decided to change his heart toward his son from anger to acceptance. He realized that he had rejected Matt due to Matt's behavior and had created, as a result, a large wall between them.

The next afternoon, Bill asked to speak to Matt regarding how he had been treating him. Bill asked Matt to forgive him for his anger and for attempting to force Matt to follow his commands. He explained to Matt that he had never honored Matt's will, or even acknowledged that Matt had a choice. He had been the rule maker and had acted as though there was only one will in the household, Bill's will. He again acknowledged this as wrong and asked Matt to forgive him. Matt said he did, but was pretty skeptical that his dad had actually changed. He needed proof.

Bill went on to talk about the recent issue regarding playing the CD and not opening the door.

He told his son, "Matt, we have granted you the privilege of having your own room in our home. However, it is important to your mother and me that we be able to sit down with you and talk when there is an issue we need to discuss. Therefore, we request that if your mother or I knock at the bedroom door when you are inside, that you open the door so we can sit down and talk. I now realize that I have always tried to force and control you and that this was wrong. I have acted as if you had no will or right to make a choice. Understanding that this is wrong, I would now like to change how I relate to you. So rather than trying to control you and being very angry with you when you refuse to be controlled, I would now like to acknowledge that you have a will and are able to make choices. Therefore, I would like to relate to you in the future by offering choices with applied consequences.

"So regarding your room, if your mother or I have something we would like to discuss with you and we come to knock on the door, you can make one of two choices. Choice A: you can either open the door and we can sit down and talk. Or, choice B: you may choose not to respond and leave the door locked, and we won't be able to talk at that time. However, there is a consequence for each choice. If you choose choice A, you will retain the privilege you now enjoy regarding your room. If you choose choice B, you will lose privilege that you now enjoy regarding your room. Do you understand?"

Matt was still not very receptive to his father, so he responded with, "Yah, whatever."

"By the way, I highly recommend choice A. I think you will enjoy retaining the privileges of your room much more than losing them," concluded Bill.

Of course two days later, Matt decided to test his dad's new strategy. He put on the same CD as before and turned it up loud. When Bill came to the door and knocked, again Matt didn't respond, but only turned the music up louder.

Bill, standing at the door, said to himself, "I think that he's chosen choice B. No problem. That is his choice."

Bill went back downstairs to read a magazine and didn't think any more about it that evening. In the morning when Matt came down to breakfast, he, of course, was expecting to be verbally assaulted by his father. However, Bill was pleasant.

"Hi, Matt," greeted Bill. "How did you sleep?"

"Fine," said Matt.

Bill continued talking about the activities of the day. Matt mentioned that he had football practice after school.

Bill commented, "You sure are an incredible football player. I wouldn't be surprised if you get a football scholarship to a major university. I sure am proud of you. I love you son. Have a great day."

Needless to say, Matt walked out of the house that morning shocked. "What happened to Dad?" he thought.

That evening when Matt returned home, Bill was sitting in the living room reading the paper.

"Hi, Matt," Bill said.

"Hi, Dad," replied Matt.

"How was school today?"

"Fine, Dad. Football practice was a little long today."

"I sure am proud of you, son. You are a great football player."

"Thanks, Dad."

Matt went on upstairs to his room. About twenty seconds later he came running back down, expressively calling to Bill.

"Dad, Dad, there's no door on my room! Just a blanket hanging where the door used to be."

"I know about that," said Bill. "Remember the talk we had a couple of days ago, in which I told you I would no longer try to force you to obey me. I mentioned that I would govern by offering choices with applied consequences?"

"Yes," said Matt.

Bill continued, "Regarding your room, I mentioned that when I knocked on the door, you could choose choice A to open the door, or choice B to keep the door locked?"

"Yes," replied Matt.

"I also told you that there would be a consequence of retaining or losing privilege regarding your room depending upon your choice. Remember last night when I knocked on your door and asked to talk with you? You chose choice B, to keep the door locked and not respond to me. If you recall, I did recommend choice A, as I thought you would enjoy that consequence more. However, you chose choice B, which is fine. It is your choice.

"But, as I mentioned, there is a consequence to each choice. I told you that you would lose privilege regarding your room. Well, apparently until now, you thought that having a door on your room was a right. But actually, it was a privilege. So for the next couple of weeks you won't be having a door on your room. If your mother or I have something we need to discuss with you, we will be able to freely talk with you."

"But Dad....," complained Matt.

Bill continued, "Matt, I just want to let you know how much I love you. You are an incredibly intelligent, gifted and talented young man. I'm so glad that you are my son. You're a blessing to me. But for the next couple weeks – no door. God bless you, son. Have a great evening."

This experience began to rebuild relationship between Bill and Matt. Bill was able to discipline his son while at the same time valuing him and honoring his will and choice. Before, when Bill was trying to control Matt, he had always stripped his son of value and humiliated him in his attempt to force his own will and control his son's behavior. By simply applying consequences of choices in exercising legitimate authority, Bill had been able to bring correction to Matt's behavior while still honoring Matt's choices and valuing him as a person. I believe that this is the same way that God governs us.

Eat the Peas

Let me give you one more example of the same principle applied in a family with small children. Have you ever tried to get little children to eat vegetables? This is not an easy chore. Parents who don't understand God's system of government oftentimes attempt to control little children and force them to eat certain foods. Because parents are physically larger, it is possible to physically force little children to obey.

For example, suppose a father is trying to get his five-year-old daughter to eat peas. He might ask kindly, then tell her that the spoon full of peas is an airplane and try to get her to open the hangar door (her mouth) and let the airplane (spoon of peas) come into the hangar. When she still refuses, perhaps he begins to get angry and begins to raise the volume and intensity of his voice. In the end, he may even physically force her mouth open and shovel in the peas. Again, this is Satan's system of control, not God's system of exercising authority.

I once heard of a very wise father who understood how to exercise legitimate authority in his home. His five-year-old daughter was sitting at the dinner table along with his wife. This father approached the table dressed in a very nice suit like a waiter, with a towel over his left arm. In his right hand he held a dish of green peas.

As he approached, he addressed his daughter and said, "Good evening, Miss. My name is Dad. I'll be your server this evening. For your dining pleasure and enjoyment, we have available this evening your choice of luscious green peas or no TV. Which would you prefer?"

The little girl said, "I hate peas. I don't want any, but I want to watch TV."

The father smiled and replied, "I'm so sorry, Miss. That order is not available this evening. You may have peas and TV, or no peas and no TV. Which would you like?

The daughter scowled and emphatically said, "No peas!"

The dad then said, "Very, well, Miss," and removed the peas.

After dinner, the little girl ran into the family room and hit the TV remote button. However, the TV did not come on. She then called to her father for help.

"Daddy, the TV doesn't work," she exclaimed.

"Oh, I'm so sorry about that," he replied. "The power has been disconnected for tonight since you chose no peas and no TV."

"But Daddy, it's my favorite program. Please!"

"No, sweetheart. Remember, your choice was no peas and no TV. I wish you would have chosen to eat the peas and watch TV, but you didn't. I love you. You are very precious to me, but no TV," he said with a smile.

Now how many times do you think that this father had to remove the power from the TV? If you guessed one time, you are right. The next week his little girl chose to eat peas and watch TV.

How many times do you think that Bill had to remove the door from Matt's room? Again, if you guessed one time, you would be correct. God's system of governing works very well and saves parents much stress, frustration, high blood pressure, etc. Utilizing God's system of government allows a parent to effectively correct the behavior of a child without devaluing, dishonoring, or attacking the identity of the child. One can discipline with a smile and a calm voice. God did not intend for a parent to be "in control," but rather to exercise legitimate delegated authority.

False Plumb Lines

I have found through years of listening to people that many hold an image of God that is very similar to the image of their father or mother. If Satan's system of control was used to govern the family during growing up years, then many times children's view of God will be the same as their view of the rule maker in the family. If Dad (or Mom, or whoever was the rule maker) was in control, then even as adults, children who grew up in that family still see God as in control. If Dad did not acknowledge or honor your will and choices, then you believe that God, likewise, does not honor your will or choices. If Dad forced his will upon those in the family, then God will force His will upon you in adult life. If Dad got angry and punished unjustly or without cause, then God will be perceived to punish unjustly.

These are actually very false images of God, but such a person believes with all his/her heart that this is who God is.

Once this belief is established, then circumstances of life seem to confirm that these images are correct. An image established in the heart while growing up is like an internal plumb line by which we measure events and circumstances of life in adulthood. We then build the wall of our personality and character each day in accordance with the plumb lines established in childhood. We even view scripture through the grid established by our own internal plumb lines.

What exactly is a physical plumb line? It is a metal weight on the end of a string that is known to always hang vertically. One can then use a plumb line to measure the verticality of a wall. It is not possible to sight with the naked eye whether a wall being constructed is vertical or not. If the wall is built without the use of a plumb line there is a significant chance that it will not be exactly vertical, and thus will lack the structural integrity to withstand wind, earth tremors, or other forces that might knock it down.

One thing worse than building a wall without a plumb line is building a wall with a perverted plumb line that does not hang truly vertical. Suppose an unseen magnet is introduced near a plumb line that draws the metal plumb bob off vertical. You then build a wall utilizing this plumb line as the standard. Obviously there is a one hundred percent chance that your wall will not be vertical and will lack structural integrity. In scripture we often see that a plumb line has to do with the images that are established in our hearts, or the way in which we process information and come to conclusions.

Through the prophet Amos, God gives Israel a graphic picture that they have built the wall of their society and established their ways using a false plumb line. The Lord now tells them that He is going to hang His true plumb line next to their crooked wall to expose what they have not yet seen.

Thus He showed me; Behold the Lord stood on a wall made with a plumb line, with a plumb line in His hand. And the Lord said to me, "Amos, what do you see?" And I said, "A plumb line." Then the Lord said: "Behold, I am setting a plumb line in the midst of My people Israel; I will not pass by them anymore." (Amos 7:7-8)

In other words, God is going to set His true plumb line along side of Israel's societal wall and show them that their wall is not straight. They have built it with a perverted plumb line that they thought was straight. Of course, the true plumb line by which to measure everything is the Bible, God's word.

I believe that today many people have built the wall of their heart using false plumb lines that were established in childhood within their family. If we are open, God will now come and hold His true plumb line up to our wall and gently begin to expose that the way we see life and interpret circumstances may not be in alignment with His true plumb line.

Family Foundations International offers weekend seminars designed to facilitate this process of experientially aligning the images in your heart with God's true plumb line. These seminars are designed to lead you through a very simple process that results in an encounter with the Holy Spirit, so that He can remove false plumb lines images at a core level and establish God's true plumb line in your heart. This initial seminar is called *An Ancient Paths Seminar: Empowering Relationships.*[2]

Reflection

1. Two Greek words are translated into the one English word, the "will" of God. These two concepts are:

   a. The unalterable purpose of God, which no man will thwart.

   b. The desire of God, which is subject to the choices of men.

2. God and Satan govern people using totally different systems of government. God offers choices with consequences. Satan forces, manipulates, threatens and controls.

3. The image of God contained in our hearts has been established through childhood experiences according to a false plumb line.

4. God is now bringing a true plumb line to our lives to help correct these false images.

5. In what area of your life do you perceive you may have one or more false plumb line images of God due to past family experience?

---

[2] For a schedule of Ancient Paths seminars near you, please visit www.familyfoundations.com

Resources

1 *An Ancient Paths Seminar*: *Empowering Relationships* or *The Ancient Paths Seminar*. See the Appendix for details. A schedule of upcoming events can be viewed on our website at www.familyfoundations.com.

chapter 3
WHAT DOES GOD LACK?

I n chapters one and two, we talked about the concept that God governs the people of the earth through the exercise of sovereign authority, but that He is not in control. We began to touch on the question of why we see such a prevalence of evil and injustice on the earth. Is this God's will? Does God really want the world to be the way that it is? We should now understand that the evil and injustice we see taking place is certainly not the "desire" will of God. Most believers would agree that there are many things going on that were never God's intention. So again the question arises: If God has power to stop the evil and injustice, then why doesn't He?

I believe that we must first understand that the evil which we desire God to stop or eliminate abides in and operates through people. Therefore, in order to rid the earth of evil, God would have to rid the earth of people. To be true to the justice of His character, God could not selectively eliminate only certain degrees of evil. Each of us is thinking, of course, "The evil in me is not as bad as the evil in others." So in order to behave in total justice, God would have to eliminate all people in whom <u>any</u> evil abides or through whom any evil works in order to justly rid the earth of evil. Of course you realize that if God were to do this, He would have to eliminate all people on the earth.

Does God have the power and ability to rid the world of evil by ridding the world of people? Absolutely! So it becomes obvious that **the presence of people and God's love for us is more valuable to Him than the absence of evil and injustice.** This is the first thing we must understand about why we see the proliferation of evil and injustice.

Furthermore, I believe that God has not just left the world to be overcome by Satan, demons, and the wickedness of men. God has implemented a plan to bring His Kingdom rule to planet earth in our time. However, I believe that there is something that God lacks in order to accomplish this and apply His government to men on the earth. You may immediately be thinking, "What could there possibly be that God lacks? He is God Almighty, omniscient, omnipotent, omnipresent. What could He lack?"

What Does God Have?

Before we look at what God lacks, let's look at what He has. God has:

1. **Knowledge:** God has all knowledge. He is not unaware of what is going on here on planet earth. God has foreknowledge of future events and choices. He knows all things. God is painfully and intimately aware of the evil and injustice on the earth. **So God certainly is aware of evil and injustice and has knowledge of all of it.**

For if our heart condemn us, God is greater than our heart, and knows all things. (1 John 3:20)

2. **Wisdom**: God is very smart and knows what to do, and when and how to do it. He is the supreme strategist. He is not incompetent, nor are His plans foolish. **God is incredibly wise and knows how to eliminate evil and injustice.**

Now unto the King eternal, immortal, invisible, to God, Who alone is wise, be honor and glory for ever and ever. Amen. (1 Timothy 1:17)

3. **Power**: God has the force necessary to accomplish any purpose He has. The battle between God and Satan is not like the light side vs. the dark side of the force in the Star Wars movies, in which the outcome of the battle is in question. It is more like the battle between an elephant and an arrogant, loud-mouthed ant. At any moment, the elephant can say, "That's enough." He raises his foot and stomps on the ant. No more ant! There is no battle between any created being and the Almighty Creator. **God has the power to eliminate evil and injustice at any moment.** God refers to Himself many times as God Almighty, the one who has all power. This word for Almighty is El Shaddai.

And God said to him, I am God Almighty: be fruitful and multiply. (Genesis 35:11)

4. **Love/Goodness**: I once heard love defined as, "choosing the highest good for all concerned." God inherently contains in His character love, goodness and a kind intent toward us. Furthermore, God always

43

acts out of His character, and never contrary to it. Thus He always chooses the highest good for all concerned. Evil and injustice are contrary to love. God's attitude toward evil and injustice is that He hates these things and is displeased with them.

So truth fails, and he who departs from evil makes himself a prey. Then the Lord saw it, and it displeased Him that there was no justice. (Isaiah 59:15)

Evil cannot abide in the presence of love. Since God is love and has love, God certainly has the desire and motive to eliminate evil and injustice.

And we have known and believed the love that God has for us. God is love, and he who abides in love abides in God, and God in him. (1 John 4:16)

What Does God Lack?

So we see that God is not lacking power, love, knowledge, or wisdom in the quest to eliminate evil and injustice. He is neither unaware, nor foolish, nor impotent, nor unconcerned regarding evil on the earth. God sees and knows what's going on; He knows how to eliminate evil and injustice; He has the power to do it; and He cares deeply and wants to do so. So why doesn't He just do it? What does He lack? God lacks one critical element necessary to get the job done. **He lacks authority.**

"Authority? How could He lack authority?" you might ask. "He is God Almighty, the One who owns everything." Let me explain the reason that God lacks authority. The very short answer is that God delegated His authority to man. I call this delegation, which occurred in the book of Genesis, <u>The Great Commission</u>. I realize that we usually refer to The Great Commission as the proclamation of Jesus over the disciples in Matthew 28. However, I like to think of this as The Great Re-commission. Let's look at the original commission in Genesis 1.

So God created man in His own image; in the image of God He created him; male and female He created them. Then God blessed them and God said to them, "Be fruitful and multiply; fill the earth and subdue it; have dominion over the fish of the sea, over the birds of the air, and over every living thing that moves on the earth." (Genesis 1:27-28)

What did God actually say and do in the commission recorded in the above scripture? God told Adam and Eve to be fruitful, multiply, fill the earth, subdue the earth and exercise dominion over every living thing on earth. Dominion is defined as supreme authority. So when God spoke to the man and woman in the Garden, He commissioned them to subdue (bring under subjection or cultivation) the earth, and to have dominion over all life on the planet. In doing so, God had to give something away. What He gave to Adam and Eve was His authority.

Let me state the obvious: If God gave His authority to man, then God no longer retains the authority. Why? Because authority is a thing that only one person can have at a time.

Thus, when God gave authority to man in the Garden, He voluntarily limited Himself in the exercise of His authority.

Let's look at a couple of other scriptural confirmations of the authority given to man.

When I consider Your heavens, the work of Your fingers, the moon and the stars, which You have ordained, what is man that You are mindful of him, and the son of man that You visit him? For You have made him a little lower than the angels, and You have crowned him with glory and honor. <u>You have made him to have dominion over the works of Your hands; You have put all things under his feet,</u> all sheep and oxen, even the beasts of the field, the birds of the air, and the fish of the sea, that pass through the paths of the seas. (Psalm 8:3-8)

The heaven, even the heavens, are the LORD's; <u>But the earth He has given to the children of men.</u> (Psalm 115:16)

In these two passages above, we see that the Lord has given authority (dominion) over the earth to men. However, God did not give up ownership or sovereignty over the earth. It is still His earth and He is still ultimately responsible for it. He created it and everything on it, and it is still His.

<u>The earth is the LORD's, and all its fullness,</u> the world and those who dwell therein. (Psalm 24:1)

46

What Happens When Sam Rents His House to Joe?

Let me employ the analogy of a lease to help us understand the interaction between God and man in Genesis 1. When a lease is signed, ownership is not given up, but authority is. For example, suppose that Sam owns a house that he would like to rent to someone for a few years. Joe desires to rent Sam's house for six years. This is agreeable to Sam, so he draws up a lease contract (Genesis 1:28, the Great Commission) which Joe signs, conveying the right to live in the house for a period of six years. Now during the term of the lease, who owns the house? Sam, of course, still owns the house. But what did Sam give to Joe in the lease? He gave him authority over the house. So Sam has voluntarily limited his access and right to determine what goes on in that house for the term of the lease.

Even though it is Sam's house and he does have a key, Sam does not have authority to enter the house without Joe's agreement. When Sam does come to the house, he must knock on the door and ask permission from Joe to gain entrance. Once inside, Sam cannot dictate where to place furniture or hang pictures, or even who may live in the house or come and go from the house. The authority to make these decisions has been delegated to Joe, even though it is still Sam's house and he owns it.

This is similar to what God gave to Adam. A suitable description would be that God leased the earth to man in Genesis 1:28. It seems that the term of the lease is probably about six thousand years, and that the lease term is almost up. We can read in the Bible what happens when the lease term is up and the Owner returns. The entire situation then changes. You may want to read **Matthew 21:33-44 and Revelation 18:11-20:6** in light of this lease analogy.

Suppose that Sam, the owner, gains knowledge from the local gas company that there is a probable gas leak in Joe's house. He then, as the landlord, wants to get that leak repaired immediately to avoid a fire or explosion, which would not only endanger Joe and his family, but also might destroy the value of Sam's property. However, Joe has no knowledge of this leak. So Sam calls a competent repairman and has him standing by to repair the leak.

Now Sam has knowledge, wisdom, power, and desire to fix the problem. However, he still cannot do so. What does he lack? He lacks authority, which he has delegated to Joe for the term of six years. He cannot enter Joe's house without Joe's permission. So Sam calls Joe by phone and apprises him of this new information about Joe's house and requests that Joe grant permission for the repairman to enter his house, find the leak and repair it. Joe, of course, is happy to do so, as he also is very aware of the danger of the situation. Joe opens the door. The repairman comes in, fixes the leak and removes the danger.

In the above example, we see that Sam must actually partner with Joe in order to repair the leak, combining his knowledge, wisdom, power and desire with Joe's authority and desire. Before Sam calls, Joe cannot repair the leak because he lacks knowledge (he doesn't know there is a leak) and power (he doesn't have the money to pay the repairman). Sam can't fix the leak because he lacks authority, and in his integrity won't violate his word given in the lease agreement. So it takes both Sam and Joe partnering together to get the job done.

In a similar way, when we as covenant disciples combine our authority with God's knowledge, wisdom, power and desire to act on earth, God's supernatural power is released to accomplish miracles. We'll discuss more about some practical aspects of how we can partner with God to release His power in a subsequent chapter on prayer.

Let's look at a further analogy. Suppose one month into the lease Joe now decides to invite a former friend, Doug, who is now a drug lord, to come live with him in his rented house. Not only that, Doug tricks Joe into subleasing the house to him, thereby relinquishing Joe's authority over the house to Doug, the drug lord. Doug now invites a couple of his other "druggie" friends to come live with them. Joe, under Doug's influence, now becomes a drug addict himself, and he and his family become slaves to Doug, who now has authority over the house. As the months progress, the situation worsens as Joe becomes deeper and deeper in debt to Doug because of his drug habit.

When Sam finds out about this situation, he is greatly distraught. This was not at all what he had in mind for Joe or for his house. However in the lease agreement, Sam has given full authority over the house to Joe for six years. Although Sam doesn't like it, he is a man of integrity and will not violate his own word that he gave to Joe in the lease agreement. However, Sam is very wise and begins to work on a plan to help Joe get free from his slavery to Doug.

Four years into the lease, Sam manages to convince Doug to sell him back the lease for an incredibly huge amount of money. Sam not only repurchases the lease, but also pays Doug the entire amount of Joe's accumulated debt. Sam then tells Joe what he has done and sends Joe through a drug rehabilitation clinic and frees him from his bondage to drugs. Sam then tells Joe, "I have now received back all authority

49

over this house. I am now giving that authority back to you. Go and tell all your other family members what I have done for you, and that the same freedom is available to them. And remember, I will be with you to help you for the rest of the term of the lease." (Matthew 28:18-20, the Great Re-Commission.)

Joe now continues to live in the house, but even though Doug no longer has authority, he and his friends refuse to leave. Unfortunately, some of Joe's family members are still greatly afraid of Doug and won't confront him. Others are still addicts and owe Doug a lot of money for drugs. A few others are actually helping Doug deal drugs and are some of his best allies. This makes life very difficult for Joe. He is constantly being undermined by some of his own family members who are afraid of or allies of Doug.

Sam, however, is very wealthy, wise and well connected. He manages to find out most of Doug's schemes even before Doug can implement them. So for the next two years until the term of the lease is up, Joe must learn how to work with Sam to combine his authority with Sam's knowledge, wealth, and wisdom to defeat the evil schemes that Doug and his allies continue to try to implement.

What Happens When God Rents His Earth to Adam?

Hopefully by now you have fully caught the drift of the analogy. The analogy doesn't carry all the way through in every area, but is adequate to convey the concept of God having delegated authority to man. In the analogy, of course, Sam is God, Joe is man, and Doug is Satan. With this understanding, let's look at what has actually happened.

God created the earth and Adam and Eve. He then delegated authority over the earth to Adam and Eve, as in a lease, (Genesis 1:28) the Great Commission. Satan then deceived Adam and Eve, and convinced them to voluntarily relinquish the authority over the earth to him. Satan then became ruler over the earth and all mankind. He then set up his kingdom of sin and death, and subjected the whole world and all mankind to it.

We know that we are of God, and the whole world lies under the sway of the wicked one. (1 John 5:19)

God was deeply grieved over this situation, but as much as He wanted to simply cancel the lease, He was bound by His own integrity to honor His own word that He had given to Adam conveying delegated authority over the earth and all life on it. God's integrity to honor His covenant word was so strong that He now actually was bound by that integrity to honor the authority of Satan on the earth. Amazing!

God then chose a particular man, Abraham, and his descendants the Hebrew people, Israel, through whom to reveal Himself to all mankind. Through Israel, God was hoping to draw all peoples back into relationship with Himself. He made a covenant with Israel and promised them that at a unique point in time He would send Messiah, His Son, who would be God incarnate and would set them free from their bondage to Satan and his kingdom. Messiah would come and establish a new covenant with the Hebrew people, the House of Israel and the House of Judah.

Behold, the days are coming, says the LORD, when I will make a new covenant with the house of Israel and with the house of Judah. (Jeremiah 31:31)

Two thousand years ago, Yeshua (Jesus), the Hebrew Messiah was born in Israel in fulfillment of God's covenant promise to Abraham, Isaac, Jacob, and their descendants. Most of us who have grown up in a Gentile Christian culture have traditionally called this Hebrew Messiah by the Greek name, Jesus. In the last couple of years, I have had a desire to honor Jesus' earthly Jewish heritage and to refer to Him by His Hebrew name, Yeshua. Whenever I meet someone from another country and culture, I like to try to pronounce their name as closely as I can to the way it is pronounced in their language. For example, when I meet a man from Mexico named Eduardo, I prefer to try to call him Eduardo, rather than Eddie. I'm sure that Jesus recognizes and responds to either name, but I beg your indulgence for the remainder of this book if I refer to the Messiah by His Hebrew name, Yeshua HaMessiach, rather than Jesus Christ.

> I have had a desire to honor Jesus' earthly Jewish heritage and to refer to Him by His Hebrew name, Yeshua.

Through His death on the cross and shed blood, Yeshua paid in full that which was necessary to receive back from Satan the authority over the earth that he had been given by Adam. Most believers have heard that Yeshua paid for and took upon Himself their sin. However, many people have not realized that when He rose from the dead, Yeshua took away from Satan the authority over the earth. It is amazing to see what He then did with that authority. Yeshua restored the authority to His Hebrew disciples in the Great Recommission.

And Jesus came and spoke to them, saying, "<u>All</u> *<u>authority has been given to Me</u> in heaven and on* *earth. Go therefore and make disciples of all the* *nations, baptizing them in the name of the Father* *and of the Son and of the Holy Spirit, teaching* *them to observe all things that I have commanded* *you; and lo, I am with you always, even to the* *end of the age." Amen.* (Matthew 28:18-20)

This New Covenant was made by the God of Abraham, Isaac and Jacob with the descendants of Abraham, Isaac and Jacob. It was consummated by the Hebrew Messiah exclusively with the Hebrew people. Authority was then restored on earth through this New Covenant and conveyed into the hands of the Hebrew partakers of the New Covenant of Messiah Yeshua. (We will discuss the concept and power of a covenant, and the authority conveyed by covenant in chapter five and six.)

God's intention, however, was to embrace in this New Covenant any people, even Gentile believers who were willing to be engrafted into the Hebrew New Covenant. Thus, the Covenant and the authority that came with it were soon extended beyond just the Hebrew people, as many Gentile believers also received and entered into this Hebrew New Covenant. In Romans 11, Apostle Paul uses the analogy of being grafted into an olive tree to explain this concept of Gentiles entering into an exclusive covenant between God and the Hebrew people.

For I speak to you Gentiles; inasmuch as I am *an apostle to the Gentiles, I magnify my* *ministry,...* Romans11:13

And if some of the branches were broken off, and you, being a wild olive tree, were grafted in among them, and with them became a partaker of the root and fatness of the olive tree, do not boast against the branches. But if you do boast, remember that you do not support the root, but the root supports you. (Romans 11:17-18)

Thus both Hebrew and Gentile believers became recipients of the authority redeemed from Satan by Yeshua. When Yeshua rose from the dead with the restored authority over the earth, this terminated Satan's legal right to function any further on the earth. The Bible tells us that actually Satan and his demonic rulers of this age were deceived, and had no idea that by crucifying Messiah they would forfeit the authority Satan had gained from Adam.

[Wisdom] which none of the rulers of this age knew; for had they known, they would not have crucified the Lord of glory. (1 Corinthians 2:8)

Now without direct authority, Satan must access authority on earth by deceiving men and women to allow him to access their authority and operate through them. Deception is the primary weapon of the kingdom of darkness. Satan and demonic forces truly have no authority or effective weapons other than deception. Unfortunately, over the last two thousand years, and certainly today, there are plenty of people on earth who are more than willing to cooperate with Satan and his kingdom to perpetrate wickedness, evil and injustice against others.

During this time in history, I believe that the primary job of New Covenant believers is to learn how to cooperate with God to use the authority Yeshua redeemed for us combined with God's knowledge and power to accomplish His Kingdom purposes on earth. This is our function until the current earth lease is up, at which time Messiah will return, instantly vanquish Satan and his allies, and establish His millennial reign on the earth.

Reflection

1. God has knowledge, power, wisdom, and love.

2. God lacks authority on earth because His authority has been delegated to man.

3. The authority and charge given to man in Genesis 1:28 can be likened to God granting man a lease over the earth for approximately 6000 years.

4. In what areas of your life have you not understood the authority that God has delegated to you? What has been the consequence of that lack of understanding?

chapter 4
OUR CURRENT BATTLE

Finally, my brethren, be strong in the Lord and in the power of His might. Put on the whole armor of God, that you may be able to stand against the wiles of the devil. For we do not wrestle against flesh and blood, but against principalities, against powers, against the rulers of the darkness of this age, against spiritual hosts of wickedness in the heavenly places. Therefore take up the whole armor of God, that you may be able to withstand in the evil day, and having done all, to stand. (Ephesians 6:10-13)

Even though a great victory was won at the cross, there is still a spiritual battle raging today. The reason this battle continues is because the vast majority of the human population has little to no relationship with God and has never entered into His covenant. Worse yet is the fact that a large majority of those who are in relationship and have entered into covenant with God by the blood of Messiah Yeshua have little awareness of the authority delegated to them, and thus have little to no understanding of what is actually taking place and how to fight the battle.

This thinking that "God is in control" renders New Covenant believers powerless as pawns, rather than warriors. Many times when the kingdom of darkness wins a coup, believers are left questioning, "Why did God (who is in control) allow that?" rather than understanding that a battle was just lost, and that they just got the tar beat out of them by the enemy. When this happens, some people do not even perceive that there was a battle and simply think that God was the author of the unjust or evil situation.

> While it is indeed true that God is an opportunist and will take advantage of every evil and unjust circumstance for your benefit, this by no means implies that God authored the circumstance.

I have heard many times people say, "Well, God allowed that in order to teach me patience, humility, or some other godly character quality." While it is indeed true that God is an opportunist and will take advantage of every evil and unjust circumstance for your benefit, this by no means implies that God authored the circumstance.

Do Firemen Start Fires?

I once heard a story about a family who lived right next to a fire station. When the alarm rang at the fire station, the father, who loved to watch the firefighters in action, would frequently get in his car and follow the fire brigade to the scene of the fire. From the time his first son was just a very little boy, this father used to take his son along with him to watch the firemen perform their heroic duties. They saw the firefighters rescue children from burning apartment buildings on tall ladders. Sometimes the men would run into a burning building and run back out carrying people in their arms, just before the building collapsed from structural failure.

It was really exciting for the little boy to see these heroic feats. The father and son continued to follow the fire trucks to the fires for several years. One day, when the boy was eight or nine years old, having been going to fires with his dad for many years, he voiced to his father a philosophical question.

"Dad," he mused, "Why do those firemen start all of those fires?"

The father, shocked and puzzled by the question, suddenly realized that for all of those years his son had been under the impression that the firemen were the ones who had started the fires so that they could then go and put out the fires and perform all of their heroic deeds.

Many people think in a similar way about God. Their logic is the same as the little boy's. Because you see God on the scene of every crisis means that God authors crises. Or, because you see firemen on the scene of every fire means that firemen start fires. God is the master of every circumstance, but God is definitely not the author of every circumstance.

What does Apostle John tell us was the purpose of the Son of God regarding the works of the devil? Was it, "The Son of God was manifested that He might change the works of the devil?" Or maybe, "The Son of God was manifested that He might speak against the works of the devil?" Or surely, "The Son of God was manifested that He might use the works of the devil to teach you something?" NO!

For this purpose the Son of God was manifested, that He might destroy the works of the devil. (1 John 3:8b)

"Destroy" is a very different concept from "use" or "teach." If Yeshua, the Son of God, came to destroy the works of the devil, and yet God is attempting to use the works of the devil to teach you something, then God and the Son of God are at odds with each other. Of course this is nonsense. The Father and Yeshua will never have purposes contrary to each other. The devil is not God's agent, but rather is God's enemy perpetrating works against humanity, which is directly contrary to the will and purposes of God. Consequently, God does not authorize or condone any of the works of the devil. The Bible tells us that Yeshua's purpose is that He might destroy every one of these evil works of the devil.

God Works All Things Together For Good

However, this does not mean that when the devil or our own foolishness succeeds in propagating some destructive work against us, that God will not work to bring blessing and benefit out of destruction and devastation. Apostle Paul told us in his letter to the Romans that God is an "opportunist," who will utilize every destructive work of the enemy to benefit and bless people.

And we know that all things work together for good to those who love God, to those who are called according to His purpose. (Romans 8:28)

Unfortunately, many well-meaning friends who believe that "God is in control" will often attempt to comfort someone who has experienced tragedy or devastation. They will do so by using this scripture and then implying that the reason God authored the devastating circumstance was to facilitate the subsequent good result. I call this "backwards theology." Backwards theology means that after a destructive work has happened, we then find the good thing that God has worked and use it to "explain" why God "allowed" or "caused" the destructive event in the first place. Thus, again, the works of the devil or our own foolishness are ascribed to God. In reality, such a comforter is saying to the person whose house just burned down, that Romans 8:28 means that the arsonist firemen set the fire for a good reason and with kind intent.

For example, suppose a man is driving along a two-lane highway and comes upon a barrier across the road and a sign that says, "Bridge out ahead! STOP! Turn right and follow detour signs." The man says to himself, "This sign doesn't apply to me. I'm certain that the construction work has not yet begun, and I don't want to drive way out of my way on the detour." So he drives around the barriers and continues down the road. Having ignored the sign, the Holy Spirit then strongly impresses upon this man's spirit a message to stop and turn around. Something is wrong and he must not proceed farther. The man, however, enamored with getting to his destination, ignores the prompting of the Holy Spirit and presses forward with great speed.

God then sends an angel, who appears as a man standing in the middle of the road, frantically waving his arms and trying to stop the driver. The driver, however, thinks this is just a hitch-hiker who is trying to harass him and drives around the angel and carries on. A half a mile later, the man drives his car right off the edge of the cliff and crashes into the ravine below. Some hikers see the crash and call 911. The driver is then airlifted by helicopter to a hospital in a nearby town, where he is treated for many broken bones and internal injuries.

Over the course of the next three weeks in the hospital, this driver has three different roommates with whom he shares the gospel and leads into covenant with the LORD. Several of the family members of his roommates come to visit, and they are also led into covenant with the LORD. The man's friends from his church come to visit him and one, using this "backwards theology," says to the driver, "Now I see why God let you drive off of that cliff. He wanted to use you, here in this hospital, to lead all of these people to Jesus." He then quotes Romans 8:28.

Now, the truth of the matter is that God had another plan for these other people to come into relationship with Him. In actuality, God was doing everything He could to stop the driver from driving off the cliff, destroying his car, and damaging his body. However, since the man was intent on ignoring the road sign, the Holy Spirit and the angel, he, in his impetuous foolishness, drove off the cliff anyway. God then, being an opportunist, worked this destructive event (which was not His idea) for good to use the man to lead others in the hospital room to the LORD.

God Gave Us a New House Debt Free

Let me share with you one other actual circumstance that I observed in the lives of my friends, Brendt and Kim, who pastor a church in a small rural town. It has been their goal over the last few years to eliminate all personal debt. Applying some wisdom and discipline, they had eliminated all debt except the mortgage on their house, and they were working toward that. Earlier this year, there was an incredible deluge of rain lasting for several days in their region. A levy broke and almost half their town was flooded.

The part of town that was flooded included the house in which Pastor Brendt and his family lived. Not only was the house flooded, but unfortunately an oil refinery lay in the path of the flood. In the course of events, one of the large oil storage tanks overflowed and dumped thousands of gallons of oil into the flood water. Consequently, many of the houses were flooded, not only with water, but with a layer of oil sitting on top of the water. Brendt and Kim's house sat under a lake of this oily water and was inaccessible for a couple of weeks. When they were finally able to return home, they found their home completely unlivable due to the damage from this oily water mixture. Miraculously, some family photos that had been left on a dining room table seemed to be unharmed. It seemed that they had somehow floated up with the water and oil, and then floated right back down onto the table, undamaged.

It was initially devastating to the family to lose most of their possessions and their home. They lived for the next several months in temporary housing provided by the U.S. government Federal Emergency Management Agency, awaiting decisions from the oil company, the insurance company, and the U.S. government as to any compensation to be made to them.

Meanwhile, they prayed and began to thank God that no one in their family or church was harmed, and that God would use this circumstance, through which the enemy meant to discourage and harm them, for blessing and benefit. After several months, payments were made to Brendt and Kim that amounted to enough to pay off the remaining mortgage on the destroyed house, and to purchase with cash another house in a different part of town that was very similar to the one they had previously owned. Although similar, this new house was larger and contained brand new carpet of the exact type for which the family had previously been saving. The net result was that, while Pastor Brendt and his family lost a few possessions in the flood, they ended up completely out of debt, with some cash left over in the bank, and owning a new, larger home free and clear with no mortgage.

Did God cause the flood? No, I don't think so. However, He acted as an opportunist, according to Romans 8:28 to work a destructive circumstance, meant to discourage and destroy Pastor Brendt and his family, for good, to bless them financially and eliminate their former debt. So I wouldn't now say to Brendt, "Oh, now I see why God let the nearby refinery and your town be flooded." No, I would rather say, "Isn't it wonderful to see that what the enemy meant to use to destroy you (the flood and destruction of your house and possessions), God redeemed to use to bless you and eliminate your debt."

If we were to say that God were in control, and that God caused the flood to bless Brendt and Kim, what would we then say to the president of the oil company, whose company may have lost millions of dollars in the flood? Should we then say, "God is a respecter of persons and He loved Brendt and Kim more than you or others, so He allowed a flood to bless them and to devastate you?" No, of course not. However, there is a reason why God, in His sovereignty, may have been able to be impartially partial to Brendt and Kim, while still operating in total justice, not being released to do the same for others. We will talk in more detail about how this may happen in a subsequent chapter on prayer.

Two Key Questions and Four Responses

I have often wondered why it is that so many believers, through this thinking that God is in control, are actually ascribing to God the works of the devil. As I have pondered this, I came to the conclusion that virtually all of us view the Bible and structure our theology through a grid of presuppositions that we don't realize we have. When evil is perpetrated against us or others close to us, there are two key questions that immediately arise in our hearts. The heart's answer to these questions determines the way we will view God and scripture. These questions were answered in our hearts when we were very little children through experiences with our parents and family members. These two key questions regarding evil are:

1) **Is God responsible for this? And,**

2) **Is this just (fair)?**

There are actually only four possible combinations of answers to these two questions. I have combined them in the following chart.

Presupposition	Is God Responsible?	Is This Just?
1.	YES	YES
2.	YES	NO
3.	NO	YES
4.	NO	NO

Let's take a specific circumstance and apply each of these presuppositions to it. Let's say that an evil man breaks into a Christian family's home. He proceeds to rape the 16-year-old daughter, and then gruesomely murder her father and mother in front of her and her little brother and sister. He then further taunts the children, steals the valuables and escapes into the night. How will the sixteen-year-old daughter interpret this horrific event? Her basic conclusion would depend upon which of each of these four presuppositions she has previously embraced in her heart. The conclusions of each are as follows:

1. **Is God responsible? YES. Is this just? YES.**

   Since God is in control, He is the author of everything that happens. Therefore He "allowed" this evil man to do this to our family and me, and God is thus responsible. Since God is the author of the circumstance and since God is always just and fair, then by definition this circumstance must be deemed as just and fair. My heart keeps telling me this was wrong, evil, not just, and unfair, but then that would mean that God is unjust or evil, which I cannot theologically accept. So even though I don't understand it and it makes no sense to me, I will conclude that "His ways are higher than my ways, and I don't understand how this can be just, but somehow it is, so I must accept this as being for my good and be OK with it."

   There is of course with this position a temptation to blame God in one's heart and hold bitterness and anger against Him, even while the mind is attempting to maintain the position that God is good and fair. So many people who hold this position end up with a large dichotomy between their mind and heart regarding God.

   This position number one is the position of a large majority of people in the Catholic and evangelical

Protestant church in the western world. This is also the position of most Muslims. (In sha' Allah!)

2. **Is God responsible? YES. Is this just? NO.**

    Since God is in control, He is the author of everything that happens. Therefore He "allowed" this evil man to do this to me and to our family, and God is thus responsible. It is obvious to me and to everyone that this act was very wrong and evil. Therefore since God allowed it, either He doesn't care, or He himself is evil. Consequently, I hate God, am angry and bitter toward Him, blame Him for the death of my parents and for what the rapist/murderer did to me.

    If a well meaning Christian now attempts to tell this girl that Jesus loves her and has a wonderful plan for her life, she may respond by saying, "Yeah, right. If your God is so loving and so powerful, then why did He allow a man to break into our house, kill my parents, violate me, and steal all of our valuables?"

    This position number two is the position taken by most of the atheistic, agnostic, unbelieving people in the western world. If you attempt to talk to the average nonbeliever in the western world about God, you will very likely get a response similar to the one above; "If God is loving and powerful, then why did *this* happen?" Everyone has his or her own personal unjust *this* that happened in life.

3. **Is God responsible? NO. Is this just? YES.**

    God is not in control and therefore is not responsible for this event. However, the event was indeed just and good. I don't know anyone who believes this. This would probably not ever be a position taken by the sixteen-year-old girl in our example. This may, perhaps, be the position of a crazy person or an insane sadist. Maybe this was Hitler's position regarding the Jews. Perhaps he thought, "God is not responsible for killing six million Jews. We are. And this is a just, right and good thing to do."

4. **Is God responsible? NO. Is this just? NO.**

God is not in control, is not a puppet master, and is not responsible for this event. God did not "allow" this evil man to kill my parents and rape me. This man did this completely contrary to the will and desire of God. Satan and the kingdom of darkness can and do access the authority given to men to do evil deeds that are diametrically opposed to the will of God. This event was one of those events authored by Satan and the kingdom of darkness. What was done was not good, just, or fair, but rather was extremely wrong, evil, and unjust. Yeshua came to destroy such works, not to "allow" such works. Therefore, in my heart I still know that God is powerful, loving, kind, and just. God hates what was done and weeps over it. The type of evil done to me was also done to Yeshua on my behalf, that He might take upon Himself my sin, pain, and grief. So God is really my only source of truth, help, healing and comfort.

This position number four is the position taken by some evangelical protestant Christians. This is the position that makes most sense to me, and the one that I have taken for my own life.

We find then that when there is an experience of devastation or evil that has happened, a person will tend to interpret that circumstance and God's involvement in it according to the presupposition already in the heart. I have found through talking with people that presupposition number one and two are really very similar in terms of heart response. In the heart of the person embracing both position number one and number two, there almost always abides a certain amount of anger, bitterness and distrust toward God for the evil experienced and observed on the earth. The primary difference is that the person embracing position number one has been able to cloak the true feelings in the heart behind a religious mindset that says, "Everything that happens must ultimately be for my good, because God is in control, and God is good." The person embracing position number two has no religious mindset to hide behind, and therefore is overtly angry and bitter toward God.

I have found that it is very difficult to convince the person in the street who has no relationship with God to give his life to the Lord. Usually the bottom line reason is that this person cannot believe that God can be trusted with his life because of the injustice of the past. Since he believes that God was responsible for the injustice of the past, he is not now willing to trust God with his life for fear of experiencing greater evil and injustice in the future. He feels it is better to manage and protect his own life rather than trust God, who is either asleep at the switch, doesn't care for him, or is Himself perverted and evil.

In ministering to many people who have taken position number one, we have found that when we get beneath the theology in the mind and the religious cloak and disclose what is truly in the heart, there is serious wounding, anger, bitterness, and most of all a deep distrust toward God. The mind wants to trust God, but because of the heart belief that God was responsible for the past evil and injustice suffered, the heart cannot trust God. Furthermore, "because God was in control," the thinking goes, "God, Himself orchestrated this circumstance for my benefit and character building." The consequence is that as much as this person now wants to trust God with her life, her heart won't let her. So she unconsciously continues to protect herself and manage her own life.

I have found that many people embracing position number one deep in their hearts not only struggle to trust God, but really have the feeling that God actually is a respecter of persons. This thinking is as follows: "He really does seem to have favorites, and I'm not one of them. I notice that He protects and blesses others far more than He does me. I probably don't deserve to be loved, blessed and protected anyway because of all my mistakes and sin. No wonder these bad things keep happening to me. God is just trying to get my attention and to discipline me and drive me to Him."

Presupposition number four says that God is not responsible because He exercises sovereign authority but is not in control. The person who embraces this position understands that God is not responsible for evil because He has delegated authority and dominion over the earth to man for a specific time period, such as is granted in a lease. Satan, demonic spirits, and wicked men now use that stolen authority to perpetrate their evil deeds on the earth, totally contrary to the will of God. Consequently, we are in an actual war and we don't win every battle during the term of the lease.

I have found that it is much easier to minister to people who have embraced presupposition number four when devastation occurs. They are not prone to blame God and struggle on a heart level to trust Him near as much as people who have embraced presupposition numbers one or two. They are not asking the question, "Why did this happen to me, God?" They already understand the nature of the war in which we are engaged, and are running to God to receive truth and healing.

The Sergeant Meant What He Said

It seems to me that many times believers who have embraced position number one above, reasoning that God is in control, unwittingly ascribe to God the destructive, devastating, and evil works of the enemy. I once thought of a military analogy that I believe quite accurately describes this thinking.

Suppose in the military, there is a sergeant training his platoon for combat. In order to adequately prepare his men to meet the enemy, the sergeant is very strict and demanding, with zero tolerance for mistakes or insubordination. Stern consequences are applied for inadequate performance or disobedience. As a result, his men make mistakes only one time. The men of the platoon grow to respect this sergeant, but also to fear him and his discipline. They realize that he is very serious about his orders.

After many weeks of training, this platoon is deployed to a live combat theater of war to face a real enemy. Several of the men soon find themselves in a foxhole pinned down facing enemy machine gun fire. Realizing the danger of the enemy, the sergeant adamantly tells his men, "Remain crouched down in this foxhole and do not stand up under any circumstance until I tell you to do so!"

Suppose a couple of these men in the foxhole really don't yet understand the war in which they find themselves and don't realize the danger from the enemy. They have not yet been able to distinguish the difference between the preparatory training they were undergoing and the actual combat they are now experiencing. Consequently, these men really don't understand the reason for the sergeant's commands, but rather only fear the sergeant's wrath for disobedience. They have no recognition or fear of the potential danger posed by the true enemy.

One of the men, after being pinned down in the foxhole for several hours, finally can't take it anymore and tells his buddy, "I have to stand up and stretch my legs."

His friend tells him, "I don't think you had better do so. Don't you remember what the sergeant told us? If you disobey his command he will really punish you."

"I don't care," says the first man. "I can't take it anymore. I have to stand up."

He proceeds to stand up, exposing himself to the enemy machine gun nest across the way. The enemy gunner immediately releases a burst from his gun and blows the standing soldier's arm right off. The man shrieks in pain and ducks back down into the foxhole, his arm stub bleeding profusely. How ridiculous would it be if after applying a tourniquet to stop the bleeding, his buddy looks at him and exclaims, "See, I told you the sergeant would punish you if you disobeyed."

The man with the missing arm now whimpers, "Yeah, that sergeant was serious. I'll never disobey him again."

Both of these men actually mistook the destructive act of the enemy for the discipline of the sergeant. Neither of them recognized that the training they had been through and the command of the sergeant was meant to spare them from the destruction of the enemy. Neither of them really knew the sergeant or his character. Apparently they didn't realize that the sergeant would never blow the arm off of one of his soldiers as a disciplinary action. Suppose there are soldiers like this in a combat zone who really don't understand the nature of combat. They have no true awareness of the enemy and therefore ascribe all of the actions of the enemy to their commander. Such an army would not win many battles and would certainly struggle with trust toward their commander.

I believe that this is how most of the believers who have embraced presupposition number one above actually relate to God and to life. It is imperative, however, that we understand that there is a true enemy and he is not a puppet of God. The battles are real and are not fixed. How then do we fight this battle? We will discuss this topic in the next couple of chapters. First, let me give you one more example illustrating why I believe that it is critical for us to understand that position four is a much more viable understanding of life than position number one.

Why Did Your Dad Electrocute You?

Suppose we have two five-year-old boys playing together at one of their homes. As the boys are playing with a coat hanger and paper clips near an electrical wall outlet, the father strictly warns the boys not to poke a paper clip or coat hanger into the wall outlet. He tells them that if he ever sees them even pretending to do so, that he will severely punish them. A few hours later, as the boys are again playing with the coat hanger, one of them says to the other, "Let's see what happens if I poke this into the outlet. I don't think anything will happen." Neither boy understands the danger and the reason the father commanded them not to do so. So one little boy pokes the hanger end into the outlet and is immediately knocked backward from the wall, falling unconscious on the floor. The other little boy begins to cry and scream, which brings the parents running.

Upon regaining consciousness in the hospital, the little boy looks up to see his parents and friend surrounding him by his bedside. His five-year-old friend then remarks to him, "Boy, your dad was serious. He sure punished you for disobeying him. He told you not to put the hanger in that hole and now look what he did to you."

Again, I believe that this story depicts very vividly the process that many people who have embraced presupposition number one go through when they are devastated. Sometimes the devastation occurs as a result of enemy activity as in the combat soldier example above. Other times it is simply a lack of understanding of the natural principles of life, such as in the story of the boys who did not understand the danger of live electric current. In both examples, the subjects simply did not understand that the command was given by the authority to spare them from the danger at hand. When the command was violated, the devastation occurred not by the authority applying a punishment, but rather as a result of the danger that the authority was attempting to have the subjects avoid.

Sometimes people don't believe that God actually electrocuted them, but rather that He stood right there by them and "allowed" them to poke the wire into the outlet. The reason God "allowed" this to happen was "to get my attention," they think.

In summary, we then see that if people do not understand that God has delegated authority to man, then they will embrace presupposition numbers one or two, rather than four. When presuppositions one or two are embraced, then such people are like the soldiers and children I described above. They believe that sergeants and fathers "are in control" of all circumstances. Through this theological grid, enemy machine gun fire in combat and electrocution from a wall plug are then interpreted as punishment from the sergeant and father, respectively for violation of their commands. Thus in life, when believers embrace in their hearts presupposition number one above, where "God is in control," the works of the enemy and the consequences of the violation of natural principles are then frequently mistaken for the discipline of God in one's life.

Reflection

1. Yeshua (Jesus) came to destroy the works of the devil, not to use the works of the devil.

2. God is an opportunist, who, although He does not author evil, will work all things together for good for those who love Him.

3. Many people, in lack of understanding, ascribe to God the works of the devil.

4. There are two key questions that greatly impact how we interpret life's experiences.

   a. Is God responsible for this circumstance?

   b. Is this circumstance just (fair)?

5. There are four possible combinations of answers to the above two questions:

Presupposition	Is God Responsible?	Is This Just?
1	YES	YES
2	YES	NO
3	NO	YES
4	NO	NO

6. From which of the above four positions do you tend to see life? How has this impacted your image of God?

chapter 5
UNDERSTANDING
BLOOD COVENANT

Before we continue on in our discussion of God's interaction with us, I believe that it is critical for us to entertain a brief discussion of the Eastern concept of blood covenant. All relationship with God is rooted in the understanding of blood covenant. This eastern concept of blood covenant is the foundational paradigm without which we cannot truly understand salvation, marriage, healing, or even life's circumstances. The authority that God delegated to man is based on God's covenant word to man. The New Covenant into which we Gentiles have been grafted is rooted in this concept of blood covenant. The Hebrew people, with whom the New Covenant was originally made, were eastern thinkers who were already very familiar with the concept of blood covenant. It was a part of their culture. However, many readers today are Gentiles who have been grafted into this covenant, but are not at all familiar with the concept of blood covenant.

So let's take a more detailed look at the eastern concept of blood covenant in order to gain an understanding of how

God functions and has always functioned in relationship to man on earth. In my book, *Two Fleas and No Dog*, I included a chapter on blood covenant as it pertains to marriage. I have quoted some of this chapter below in order that we might gain a better understanding of how eastern people understand and enter into blood covenant.

What Is a Blood Covenant?[1]

The Bible is set in an eastern context, and much of the biblical presentation of God's relationship with man is couched in covenant terminology. Actually, I don't think that one can truly understand the Bible without understanding the concept of covenant. Covenant (often times referred to as 'blood covenant') is an eastern or tribal concept, which has been known and practiced for centuries in the East, but is neither known nor understood in the 'civilized' West. If you had grown up in a tribal culture in Africa, North or South America, the Middle East, or Polynesia, you would probably still be somewhat familiar with the concept of covenant.

However, most of us have never seen anyone amongst our family or friends cut veins in their hands or arms, commingle the blood, drink the mixture and swear allegiance to one another unto death. The closest most of us have come to the concept of covenant is watching Geronimo make a blood covenant with another native Indian chief on TV when we were children. We then

---

[1] Hill, Craig. *Two Fleas and No Dog*. Littleton: Family Foundations International, 2007. pp 36-44

pricked our own finger with a friend and mixed the blood in order to become 'blood brothers.' In actuality, in our modern western culture, the value of covenant has by and large been exchanged for the value of contract. Our legal profession has made us familiar with this concept of contract. But what then is a covenant?

A blood covenant is a solemn agreement made between men in the presence of the deity in whom they believe, which can only be broken by death. Simply put, covenant is a promise that is broken only by death. The primary characteristics of a blood covenant are: unilateral, unconditional and irrevocable. I realize that there are many covenants in the Bible that are indeed conditional. However, we are talking here about the type of covenant that we have with God by the blood of Jesus Christ, which is depicted on earth by the marriage rela-

> A blood covenant is the closest, most sacred, most enduring, binding agreement

tionship between husband and wife. The New Covenant by the blood of Jesus is indeed unilateral, unconditional, and irrevocable.

A blood covenant is the closest, most sacred, most enduring, binding agreement known to men. A covenant is virtually never broken by those who understand and practice blood covenanting. It is such a sacred commitment for which a man or woman would die before dishonoring himself in breaking his word. In the East, a man's word in a vow or covenant is more valuable than his own life. A free man values his word above his life, while a "flea" man always values his own survival above all else, including his word. It is said that in the 19th century if a man ever broke a covenant in Africa, even his own relatives would help hunt him down to kill him. He and his offspring would be hunted and killed for up to four generations for covenant breaking. I have heard it said that among North American native peoples, a covenant breaker would be hunted and killed for up to seven generations.

The reason that it is so important for us to understand the serious nature of a covenant is that such thinking has all but disappeared from our western society today. A man's word has become quite meaningless today in much of society. Whereas in past times a covenant thinker would rather die than break his word, today a man would rather break his word than be inconvenienced to miss lunch.

I find that it is difficult today for people to understand that God is a covenant keeper and will keep His word. Most people can't relate to God keeping His word because they have no legitimate picture in human experience of someone who would keep his word even to his own detriment. In which segment of society should we look to see such an example? In the realm of politics? I read in history that there was a time in which a politician felt an obligation to fulfill his campaign promises no matter what the cost. In most countries, this is not common today.

How about in business? Again, there was a time in past history when a man gave his word that you could rely upon it. If he said it, he would do it, and a handshake was a reliable commitment. Today, a major part of the legal profession is engaged in writing agreements to try to bind men to their words. However, if a man has no value in his heart for his own word, the length and detail of the written agreement will not bind him. He will find a way to break his word and do what he wants.

H. Clay Trumbull, a biblical and anthropological scholar, wrote a fascinating book in the late 1800s entitled *The Blood Covenant*. In this work, Dr. Trumbull expounds upon the cultural traditions of blood covenanting in virtually every culture of the world. It was his thesis that God placed such traditions in each culture to prepare every people group in the world to understand the New Covenant that God has made with man by the shedding of the blood of His Son, Jesus Christ. Below, I would like to quote a couple brief passages from Dr. Trumbull's book to give you an idea of how men in the past have made blood covenants with each other.

'In bringing this rite of the covenant of blood into new prominence, it may be well for me to tell of it as it was described to me by an intelligent native Syrian, who saw it consummated in a village at the base of the mountains of Lebanon.

It was two young men, who were to enter into this covenant. They had known each other, and had been intimate (he does not mean sexually) for years; but now they were to become brother-friends, in the covenant of blood. Their relatives and neighbors were called together in the open place before the village fountain to witness the sealing compact. The young men publicly announced their purpose and their reasons for it. Their declarations were written down in duplicate—one paper for each friend—and signed by themselves and by several witnesses. One of the friends took a sharp lance, and opened a vein in the other's arm. Into the opening thus made he inserted a quill through which he sucked the living blood. The lancet-blade was carefully wiped on one of the duplicate covenant papers, and then it was taken by the other friend, who made a like incision in its first user's arm, and drank his blood through the quill, wiping the blade on the duplicate covenant-record. The two friends declared together, "We are brothers in a covenant made before God: who deceiveth the other, him will God deceive." Each blood-marked covenant-record was then folded carefully, to be sewed up in a small leathern case, or amulet, about an inch square; to be worn thenceforward by one of the covenant-brothers, suspended about the neck, or bound upon the arm, in token of the indissoluble relation"[2] (See Exodus 13:16).

Dr. Trumbull further states: 'He who has entered into this compact with another, counts himself the possessor of a double life; for his friend, whose blood he has shared, is ready to lay down his life with him, or for him.'[3] Dr. Trumbull then refers to the scripture verse, Proverbs 18:24' *A man of many friends comes to ruin, but there is a friend who sticks closer than a brother.* This scripture is obviously referring to a blood-covenant brother, as Dr. Trumbull has just described. Jonathan and David made such a covenant with each other as recorded in 1 Samuel 18.

Now it came about that when he had finished speaking to Saul, that the soul of Jonathan was knit to the soul of David, and Jonathan loved him as himself. And Saul took him that day and did not let him return to his father's house. Then Jonathan made a covenant with David because he loved him as himself. And Jonathan stripped

---

[2]Trumbull, H. Clay. *The Blood Covenant.* Kirkwood: Impact Books Inc. 1975. pp.5-6
[3]Trumbull, H. Clay. *op. cit.* p.7

himself of the robe that was on him and gave it to David with his armor, including his sword and his bow and his belt'" (I Samuel 18:1-4).

These types of understandings still exist in oriental and Middle Eastern cultures today. This is why it is still such a serious matter in many countries for an Arab Muslim to become a Christian. In their way of thinking, the man is in covenant through Islam with Allah and his brothers. In becoming a Christian, according to eastern thinking, a man is breaking this covenant with Allah and his brothers and thus is worthy of death. In many cultures, his own mother is sworn to seek his death. Since covenant is an unconditional, irrevocable, indissoluble commitment breakable only by death, covenant breaking in the East is virtually always punishable by death. When men made such a covenant with each other, they made a commitment to each other more valuable than even their own lives. When entering into such a covenant, they made the basic commitment to each other that 'all I have and all I am is yours. Your enemies are my enemies, and I am ready to give up even my life for you, if need be.'

It is an astounding thing that Almighty God would make covenant with man, committing all He is and all He has to us. Jesus Christ took upon Himself the punishment for our covenant breaking in His establishment of the New Covenant, and offered to all who will receive an irrevocable, indissoluble covenant commitment.

Covenant Is Not Dependent Upon Performance

The concept of covenant then, is a unilateral, unconditional, irrevocable, commitment before God, valid until death. Covenant does not depend upon the performance of either party. Covenant is a unilateral commitment made to another party in the presence of God and is independent of the performance of the other party.

This means that if a man gave his word in covenant, his fulfillment of that word was not dependent upon whether the other man fulfilled his word or not. It was a unilateral commitment before God. In other words, each man had chosen in advance to live a free life, not dependent upon the choices of others, but rather dependent upon unilateral choices and commitments made before God. Because of this understanding, it was very rare for an eastern man to ever break a covenant. If someone did, the entire society was outraged and all were committed to impose upon the covenant breaker the penalty for such behavior, death. It is amazing to note that in ancient Israel, even when a covenant was entered into with purposeful deceit, the covenant vow was still kept. Even after the deceit was discovered, the honorable men of Israel still fulfilled their covenant vow to a deceitful heathen nation. This story is recorded in the ninth chapter of the book of Joshua.

God had instructed Joshua and the Israelites to eliminate from the land all the Canaanites living there. They had already totally annihilated the cities of Jericho and Ai, and were now nearing the Canaanite city of Gibeon. The Gibeonites had heard what had been done to Jericho and Ai and were greatly frightened. The elders of the city devised a plan to deceive Joshua, and induce him to enter into a covenant of peace with them. They knew that if they could get the Israelites to enter into a covenant with them, Israel would then be bound to do them no harm.

The Gibeonites sent an envoy to the Israelite camp with worn-out shoes and clothing, stale bread, and cracked and mended wineskins to make it appear as if they had traveled a very great distance. They arrived and appeared before Joshua in this condition and sought to enter into a covenant of peace, saying that they were not inhabitants of the land of Canaan, but rather lived a very great distance away. Joshua and the elders of Israel did not seek the counsel of the Lord, but rather believed the Gibeonites and cut a covenant of peace with them. Only three days later, Joshua discovered that the Gibeonites had deceived him and were occupants of the land of Canaan. Although all of Israel would have liked to destroy the Gibeonites, Joshua and the leaders prevented them because of the covenant which was made with them.

So the men of Israel took some of their provisions and did not ask for the counsel of the Lord. And Joshua made peace with them and made a covenant with them, to let them live, and the leaders of the congregation swore an oath to them. And it came about at the end of three days after they had made a covenant with them, that they heard that they were neighbors and that they were living within their land. Then the sons of Israel set out and came to their cities on the third day. Now their cities were Gibeon, and Chephirah and Beeroth and Kiriath-jearim. And the sons of Israel did not strike them because the leaders of the congregation had sworn to them by the Lord, the God of Israel. And the whole congregation grumbled against the leaders. But all the leaders said to the whole congregation, 'We have sworn to them by the Lord, the God of Israel, and now we cannot touch them. Thus we will so do to them, even let them live, lest wrath be on us for the oath which we swore to them. (Joshua 9:14-19)

Despite the fact that it was a covenant that was never meant to be and even was entered into through fraud and deception, once it was made, the Israelites were bound to honor their word. Joshua and his leaders understood the issue of covenant and its value before God. They could not break their covenant even though it was made in deception with heathen Canaanites whom God had commanded the Israelites to destroy.

Joshua's concept of covenant was so strong that not only did he preserve the Gibeonites, but in Joshua chapter ten, he and the Israelites fought alongside the Gibeonites to help defeat the enemies of their covenant partners. God so honored the value of this covenant that He placed it even above the individual welfare of His chosen people Israel. In II Samuel chapter 21, a famine had been released upon Israel. When King David inquired of the Lord as to the cause of the famine, the Lord informed him that it was a result of King Saul's violation of the covenant by putting the Gibeonites to death. The famine was terminated only as King David went to the Gibeonites and repented and made restitution for the rebellious acts of former King Saul. We see here again the incredible value God places on covenant as He honors and calls Israel to honor a covenant that should have never been made in the first place.

When you make a vow to God, do not be late in paying it, for He takes no delight in fools. Pay what you vow. " (i.e. Ananias & Sapphira, Acts 5) *It is better that you should not vow than that you should vow and not pay. Do not let your speech cause you to sin and do not say in the presence of the messenger of God that it was a mistake. Why should God be angry on account of your voice and destroy the work of your hands?* (Ecclesiastes 5:4-6)

Covenant vs. Contract[4]

A covenant is a unilateral, irrevocable, indissoluble commitment before God and valid until death or even into succeeding generations. A covenant is not dependent upon the choices of another, but is a commitment unto death before God.

Let's now contrast this with the concept of a contract. The concept of contract is an entirely different concept. A contract is a bilateral agreement between two parties totally dependent upon performance of the agreement, and breakable by either party upon non-performance of the other. Under a contract, if one party fails to perform according to the contract, the other party has no obligation to perform either and is no longer bound by the terms of the contract. The following chart illustrates the contrast.

---

[4] Hill, Craig. *Two Fleas and No Dog. op. cit.* pp 49 - 52

Covenant	Contract
Unilateral	Bilateral
Unconditional	Conditional
Irrevocable	Revocable
Indissoluble	Dissoluble

A covenant is based upon the WORD of the one making the covenant, while a contract is based upon the PERFORMANCE (works) of the other party making the contract. The best word we have in English that means a covenant is a promise. A promise is based on the word of the one making the promise. If the promise maker is a person of integrity, then that promise will be kept regardless of the circumstances.

A covenant says, "I will keep my word and do what I said, whether you do or not." A contract says, "If you keep your part of the agreement, I will keep my part of the agreement. However, if you fail to keep your word, I am released and no longer obligated to keep my word."

Gift vs. Sale

Let me further illustrate this point with an example regarding a car. Suppose that I make an agreement to sell Joe my car for $10,000. Joe has the money and wants the car, and I have the car and want the money. We make a contract to exchange Joe's money for my car.

Now suppose Joe only pays me $5,000; am I obligated to give him the car? Of course not! The reason I am not is that Joe did not fulfill his end of the agreement. He didn't give me the full amount of money that he promised. On the other hand, if Joe gives me the full $10,000, what if I want to keep the money and the car? Can I do this? No! If he gives me the money, I must give him the car. Virtually any judge in any country will uphold such an agreement. So if Joe keeps his word, I must keep mine. However, if Joe does not keep his word and fulfill his end of the agreement, then I am released from fulfilling my end of the agreement. This is a contract.

A covenant, on the other hand, is a promise that is independent of the actions of the other party. Suppose instead that I tell Joe, 'Joe, because I love you like my own brother, I want to give you my car as a gift. I will make arrangements next week to have my car sent to you. I hereby promise you my car as a gift.' Now, what must Joe do to receive the car? Nothing. Simply say, 'Thank you.'

Now suppose in the ensuing time, Joe becomes offended with me for some other reason and begins telling people lies about me. Suppose he is calling many of my acquaintances and telling them that he knows for certain that I am a drug dealer and adulterer. Another friend advises me of this situation and I am shocked and hurt. Suppose I then call Joe and ask him about this and find that he is indeed offended and has no intention of ceasing his lies about me.

When confronted, Joe refuses to change. The question now is, do I still have to send him my car? Joe is not treating me as a friend, why should I send him my car? The answer is: I must send him my car because I gave him my word, and if I am a person of integrity, I will fulfill my word because I made Joe a promise. My word is my word independent of any choices, actions or attitudes that Joe might have. I will fulfill my word and keep my promise whether Joe does or not and independent of any way in which Joe treats me. This is a covenant.

Perhaps you can see already that much of our society has lost the meaning of covenant, the value of a promise, or the integrity of a person's word. This is not just in the arena of marriage, but in many areas of life. Words have become meaningless and unreliable. This is highly unfortunate because basic trust is rooted in the integrity of a person's word. I'm sure that each of us can think of many people around us who have let us down, by not honoring their word to us. However, it really is indicative of "flea" thinking to focus on all the other people who have dishonored their word. The free man looks to see if he is truly a person of integrity who keeps his word, or in what areas has he been one who has let his word be dependent upon circumstances or the choices of other people.

God Honors His Word

In understanding covenant, one of the key things that we are to understand, is that an eastern covenant thinker values his word even above his own life. God of course is the author of eastern covenant thinking, and thus He values His word supremely. Below is an incredible statement about the way in which God values His own word.

I will worship toward Your holy temple, And praise Your name. For Your lovingkindness and Your truth; For You have magnified Your word above all Your name. (Psalm 138:2)

This is an incredible statement, that God magnifies His word even above His own name. From a Hebrew frame of reference, a person's name represents his being. Their name is who they are. One eastern proverb declares, "You cannot know a man until you know his name." So for God to magnify His word above His name means that He values His word so much, He considers His word even above Himself. It means that He, Himself even bows and submits to His own word. This means that if you know what God has said, you know what God will do. He will always do exactly what He said in His word that He would do.

> So for God to magnify His word above His name means that He values His word so much, He considers His word even above Himself.

For a much more in-depth study on applying the eastern concept of Blood Covenant to our lives today, you might want to listen to my audio CD series entitled *Secrets of the Blood Covenant*[5]

A Covenant You Don't Know About Can't Help You

Let's look at an example in scripture of the covenant made between David and Jonathan, the son of Saul. This is a good example of the strength of a covenant made between two eastern covenant thinkers. Many times in the Bible, the character of David is also very representative of the heart of God. David's heart in covenant represents the heart of God the Father in covenant toward us. Let's look at the covenant that David made with Jonathan and its impact upon the next generation.

---

[5] Hill, Craig. *The Secrets of the Blood Covenant*. Littleton: Family Foundations International. 2001

Then Jonathan and David made a covenant,
because he loved him as his own soul, and
Jonathan took off the robe that was on him and
gave it to David, with his armor, even to his
sword and his bow and his belt. (1 Samuel 18:3-4)

Even after Jonathan's father, King Saul, sets his heart to
kill David, Jonathan and David reaffirm their covenant with
each other two chapters later.

And you shall not only show me the kindness of
the LORD while I still live, that I may not die;
but you shall not cut off your kindness from my
house forever, no, not when the LORD has cut off
every one of the enemies of David from the face of
the earth." So Jonathan made a covenant with the
house of David, saying, "Let the LORD require it
at the hand of David's enemies." Now Jonathan
again caused David to vow, because he loved him;
for he loved him as he loved his own soul. (1 Samuel
20:14-17)

In this passage, we see that Jonathan and David have made
a covenant similar to the two Lebanese men that Dr.
Trumbull described earlier. David has vowed to Jonathan
that he will treat the future descendants of Jonathan with
kindness and look after them, even if Saul and his family
members become David's enemies.

Let's now progress a few years forward to a time after the
death of Jonathan and King Saul. David is now becoming
king of Israel. Traditionally, in those times, whenever a new
king was coroneted, if he was not from the family of his
predecessor, he would search for and execute all members of

the former king's family. He did so to insure that there would be no descendants of the former king making a claim to the throne in the future. This practice, of course, became a great threat and fear to any living descendants of the previous king.

However, as we saw before, David had made a covenant with Jonathan to protect and bless his offspring. However, this fact apparently was not known by anyone in the household of Jonathan. So we read in Second Samuel chapter four about a son of Jonathan, named Mephibosheth, who was a little boy when his father was killed and David became king.

Jonathan, Saul's son, had a son who was lame in his feet. He was five years old when the news about Saul and Jonathan came from Jezreel; and his nurse took him up and fled. And it happened, as she made haste to flee, that he fell and became lame. His name was Mephibosheth. (2 Samuel 4:4)

We read here that Mephibosheth was dropped by his nurse as a little boy, probably in her haste to flee with others of the household of Saul when news came that David would be king. The natural expectation was that the new king, David, would hunt down any of the descendants of King Saul and kill them. Mephibosheth was thus crippled when he was dropped in haste to flee the city.

Mephibosheth, until he was five years old, lived a life of luxury in the king's palace. He was next in line to become king after his father, Jonathan. However, due to David becoming king, all of that had changed. We can only imagine the bitterness and anger that Mephibosheth probably grew up with. His family fled to a wilderness location called Lo

Debar, which in Hebrew means "place of no pasture" or "no greenery." This was a hiding place in the desert. Most likely, Mephibosheth blamed King David for his being crippled, living in a shack in the wilderness instead of in the palace in Jerusalem, and living in poverty instead of as the son of a king.

However, worse than living in these conditions, Mephibosheth considered himself a refugee. The thought that no doubt terrorized him was that one day King David might find him, bring him to Jerusalem, publicly torture and humiliate him and then kill him. (This is what kings usually did in those days with the families of their enemies.) Then suddenly, one day, Mephibosheth's worst nightmare became a reality. News came that the king's chariots were on the way to Lo Debar and that Mephibosheth had been betrayed and discovered. He tried to escape, but being crippled, he didn't get very far. The king's soldiers found him, loaded him into a carriage and conveyed him back to the city to the king's palace.

Now all this time, Mephibosheth was actually the beneficiary of a covenant that his father, Jonathan, had made with David. However, Mephibosheth had no knowledge of this covenant. Consequently, he had all of his life since age five misjudged and misunderstood the heart of King David. While he had blamed David for all the things wrong with his life, and thought that David wanted to humiliate, harm and kill him, the truth was that David only wanted to receive, love and bless him. Because Mephibosheth was a stranger to the covenant of his father with David, he had needlessly lived in hiding and in poverty in Lo Debar for many years, with no idea that he could have been living as one of the king's own sons in the palace.

It seems that the belief in Mephibosheth's mind is very similar to the belief that many people have about God. They have no understanding that Yeshua shed His blood to make a covenant available to them, and thus they are strangers to that covenant and its promises. However, because of their behavior and rebellion against God, He should rightfully be looking upon them as His enemies. Due to their own guilt, they, of course, feel like God's enemies, and are fearful, and indeed convinced that this is the way He sees them. In reality, however, because of the covenant made by Yeshua on their behalf, God, like King David, is only seeking to return them to the palace, forgive them and treat them as He would one of his own sons. Without knowledge of this, many continue to live in poverty and hiding in their own "Lo Debar" hoping that God won't find them.

Now David said, "Is there still anyone who is left of the house of Saul, that I may show him kindness for Jonathan's sake?" (2 Samuel 9:1)

We see here that the covenant that David made with Jonathan many years ago is still strong in David's heart. His only desire is to honor his covenant promise to Jonathan to bless and care for any of Jonathan's remaining descendants. Ziba, a former servant of Saul's, then informs King David that there is a son of Jonathan named Mephibosheth living in Lo Debar. David then sends for Mephibosheth, who appears now before King David. Let's look at the interaction between them.

Now when Mephibosheth the son of Jonathan, the son of Saul, had come to David, he fell on his face and prostrated himself. Then David said, "Mephibosheth?"

And he answered, "Here is your servant!" So David said to him, "Do not fear, for I will surely show you <u>kindness for Jonathan your father's sake,</u> and will restore to you all the land of Saul your grandfather; and you shall eat bread at my table continually." Then he bowed himself, and said, "What is your servant, that you should look upon such a dead dog as I?" And the king called to Ziba, Saul's servant, and said to him, "I have given to your master's son all that belonged to Saul and to all his house. You therefore, and your sons and your servants, shall work the land for him, and you shall bring in the harvest, that your master's son may have food to eat. But Mephibosheth your master's son shall eat bread at my table always." Now Ziba had fifteen sons and twenty servants. Then Ziba said to the king, "According to all that my lord the king has commanded his servant, so will your servant do."

"As for Mephibosheth," said the king, <u>"he shall eat at my table like one of the king's sons.</u> (2 Samuel 9:6-11)

What is amazing about this interaction is how the lack of knowledge of covenant had kept Mephibosheth in bondage for many years and kept him in bitterness and anger toward King David, the very one who had the power and desire to help him. This is truly the consequence of Mephibosheth's literally being a stranger from the covenant made by his father with David, many years before. I have found that there are many believers who are grafted into the New Covenant, but in reality are still strangers from it. We will examine

96

further implications of being a stranger from covenant in the next chapter.

Reflection

1. Blood covenant is the most solemn agreement known to man and is the foundation of salvation, marriage, healing, and faith.

2. A covenant is dependent upon the one who made the covenant, while a contract is dependent upon the works of another person.

3. God is a covenant keeper, who does not act randomly, but always keeps His word.

4. Contrast between a covenant and a contract:

Covenant	Contract
Unilateral	Bilateral
Unconditional	Conditional
Irrevocable	Revocable

5. King David in his relationship with Jonathan's crippled son, Mephibosheth, depicts God's desired covenant relationship with us.

6. In His interaction with you in your life, have you viewed God as acting randomly and unexplainably, or have you viewed God as a covenant keeper acting in accordance with His word and His character?

Resources

Two Fleas and No Dog (Book or Audio Book)

Secrets of the Blood Covenant (6 CDs)

chapter 6
STRANGERS FROM THE
COVENANT

Therefore remember that you, once Gentiles in the flesh—who are called Uncircumcision by what is called the Circumcision made in the flesh by hands that at that time you were without Christ, being aliens from the commonwealth of Israel <u>and strangers from the covenants of promise</u>, having no hope and without God in the world. But now in Christ Jesus you who once were far off have been brought near by the blood of Christ. (Ephesians 2:11-13)

In this above passage Apostle Paul tells us that before we were grafted into the New Covenant, we were aliens, and strangers from the covenants of promise. One day many years ago, I heard the Holy Spirit tell me, "Son, in many areas, even though you are now in covenant, you are still a stranger to the covenant."

Over the next couple weeks, I was seeking God regarding why He said I was a stranger to the covenant and how I could change. I was beginning to realize that although I was adopted and grafted into the New Covenant, I didn't really understand God's ways, or my privileges or responsibilities in that covenant. This is what made me a stranger.

The Power Is In the Shoes

About the same time that I was pondering why the LORD had spoken to me about His covenant, I happened to see on TV the old classic movie with Judy Garland, *The Wizard of Oz.* Now, before you get offended, let me say that I am not recommending this movie, nor do I believe that the theology expressed in the movie is biblical or in any way accurate. However, while watching the movie, I was powerfully impacted by the Holy Spirit with one particular point. Most believers wander through life much like Dorothy wandered through Oz, not knowing how to accomplish their purpose, while all the time having the authority to release the power to do so.

In the story, the young woman, Dorothy, while in the land of Oz, had one purpose: To return home to Kansas. However, she didn't know how to do so. The first people she met (Munchkins) told her that if she could just get to the Emerald City and have an audience with the Wizard, he had the wisdom and power to get her home. I liken this to the situation of many believers. In reality, they are chasing after "wizards." They know that they should be walking in God's supernatural power and be living the life of New Covenant believers described in the book of Acts. However, they don't know how to do so. Others then tell them, if you can just get to Toronto, or Pensacola, or Redding, or go to "brother so and so's" meetings, the "wizard" there can help you accomplish this goal. I'm not saying that we should not go to these places or meetings. I enjoy them and benefit from them as much as anyone, and do recommend going. I am simply saying that I have not found that any man or woman, city, church, or meeting holds the key to the release of God's supernatural power in our lives.

Dorothy accumulated a few traveling companions along the way, and together they made their way to the Emerald City. After fighting some battles and initially being rejected by the Wizard's doorkeeper, they were finally granted an audience with the Wizard of Oz, himself. He of course had no actual power to help Dorothy get back to Kansas, but not wanting to admit that, he sent them on a dangerous mission to bring back the broomstick of the wicked witch. The Wizard of course hoped that they wouldn't return.

At great risk to their lives, Dorothy and her friends finally did kill the wicked witch and returned to the Wizard with her broomstick, as requested. In great anticipation of finally realizing their dreams, Dorothy and her friends were sorely disappointed to find out that the Wizard was a fraud and had no real power to help her return to Kansas. Of course Dorothy and her friends had learned many very valuable life lessons on the journey, but she was no closer to returning to Kansas than when she started.

In the end, Glenda, the "good witch," shows up and reveals to Dorothy that the power to return to Kansas is actually in "the Ruby slippers." I liken this to the fact that the power to live the life that God intended for us is already contained in the New Covenant promises.

Now, think about this: When did Dorothy receive the Ruby Slippers? When she arrived in Oz. So when could she have returned to Kansas? At any time. The power was in the shoes to return home. However, what good did that power in the Ruby Slippers do her? None whatsoever. Why not? Because of two reasons. First of all, she didn't know that there was any power in the shoes. Secondly, she didn't know how to access the power in the shoes. For Dorothy, the entire time she was in Oz she had the power of the Ruby Slippers, but lived just like everyone else who had no Ruby Slippers. The moment that Glenda revealed to her the knowledge of those two facts, Dorothy then used the authority of her words to access the supernatural power in the shoes and immediately returned home. (Again, I am not saying that I believe that this power in the slippers was from God or that there is such a thing as a "good witch." I am well aware that all witchcraft is evil and from Satan, not from God. I am just utilizing the story as an analogy to make a point about our lives.)

Many believers practically live their lives just like Dorothy in Oz, totally ignorant of what is available to them in the New Covenant. Either they don't know the terms of the Covenant and what are their privileges and responsibilities, or they do know, but are ignorant as to how to access God's covenant wisdom and power. Consequently, such persons live on planet earth just like everyone else who has never entered into any covenant with God at all. For all practical purposes, the New Covenant is of no greater benefit on this earth to the recipient than the Ruby Slippers were to Dorothy during her entire stay in Oz.

What's In the Ticket?

To further illustrate the point, let me relate to you below another story I heard regarding the value of knowing and understanding what you have. This is the story of a young Scottish man in the late 1800s. His lifelong dream had been to leave Scotland to come to the United States of America to seek his fortune. Having saved his money for years, and selling all of his possessions, he finally had accumulated enough money to book passage on an ocean liner to America.

Unfortunately, the young Scotsman had spent virtually all of his money just to book the passage, and had only a little left to start his new life in America. Not having any additional money with which to purchase any meals onboard the ship, he took with him some bread, dried meat and cheese to sustain him on his voyage.

Finally, the day of departure arrived. His friends all came down to the pier to see him off. The gigantic ship's horn sounded and his voyage began. Every day that passed, the Scotsman drew closer to the fulfillment of his dream to come to America. Each day he walked past a couple of the ship's beautifully appointed restaurants. Through the windows he watched the well dressed passengers sit inside and partake of the luscious seven course meals offered to them. Often he thought that maybe he should have waited just a little longer before embarking on his journey, until he could have accumulated enough money to be able to pay for some of the meals in the ship's restaurants. But then he remembered he was on his way to America to make his fortune. Nice meals could wait. He would then go back to his cabin and partake of his bread, cheese, dried meat and water.

On the final day at sea, the young Scotsman suddenly heard shouting and a great commotion toward the bow of the ship. As he ran forward to see what was happening, he realized that the people had sighted land and the Statue of Liberty was coming into view as the ship was nearing Ellis Island in New York. Up on deck, the Scotsman got to talking to one of the ship's stewards who was asking him how he had enjoyed his trip. The passenger remarked that it had been his life-long dream to come to America, and that the trip had been wonderful. He further remarked that he only regretted not having enough money to visit any of the fine restaurants onboard and partake of any of the sumptuous meals he had seen.

A shocked look came across the steward's face as he requested, "Sir could I please see your ticket?" As the Scotsman dug his ticket out of his coat pocket and handed it to the steward, he wondered why the steward would now ask to see his ticket.

The steward, after quickly glancing at the ticket, shook his head from side to side and remarked, "Sir, didn't you realize? All of the meals were included in your ticket! You were welcome to dine with all of the other guests at each meal."

The Scotsman grabbed his ticket from the steward and ran toward the main restaurant to see what might still be available within the next half hour before they arrived at port. The obvious point of the story is that, although the Scotsman was indeed a passenger of the cruise line, he failed to understand what was included with his ticket. I realized that while I was a partaker of the New Covenant, I was not really aware of what was included in the ticket. Just as this Scotsman was a stranger to the "covenants of promise" of his ticket, I was a stranger to the "covenants of promise" of the New Covenant.

In order for a covenant to benefit you, I have discovered that the following three things must be true:

1. **You must <u>receive the covenant</u> and be an active partaker in it.**

2. **You must <u>know the privileges and responsibilities</u> of the covenant.**

3. You must be willing to <u>enforce the terms</u> of the covenant against enemies.

The Ticket You Never Bought Won't Help You

Regarding the New Covenant with God, there are many rights, privileges, and responsibilities that go along with this covenant. As I mentioned earlier, this covenant was made between God and the Hebrew people and was ratified by the blood of Messiah Yeshua (Christ Jesus). However, now God has offered an invitation to all people, whether Jewish or not, to be grafted into the Hebrew olive tree and become partakers of this covenant.

Regarding point number one above, an offer that is not received is of no benefit or value. In other words, the blood of Yeshua is not effective to forgive your sin and iniquity if you have never entered into the covenant that God has offered you.

I quoted in the last chapter a passage from Dr. H. Clay Trumbull's book on blood covenant regarding two young Lebanese men making a covenant and exchanging their lives with one another. God has also offered to do exactly this, exchange His life with yours. You give Him 100% of your life, and He gives you 100% of His life. This is an offer to enter into an eternal covenant with God, whereby you receive the following three benefits: 1) forgiveness for all of your sins; 2) a regenerated spirit, whereby you will live forever with God in His Kingdom; and 3) His authority to represent Him and His Kingdom here, now, on earth. However, this offer is of no benefit to you, if you have never received it.

Unfortunately, I have met many people who honestly think that by simply "believing" that there is a covenant, they have somehow entered into it. This would be similar to the Scotsman described above saying, "Because I believe in a ticket on an ocean liner to America, I now have that ticket and will automatically arrive in America." Of course, this is nonsense and is simply not true.

It was not enough for the Scotsman to believe that a ticket was available for him to go to America. The availability or the offer of the ticket was of no value to the man if he were not willing to make the exchange of his money for the ticket. He had to actually make the commitment to sell his possessions and exchange the sum total of his life in Scotland (now changed into money) for the ticket to America.

Many times people, and even churches, talk about the New Covenant, but never actually enter into it. I grew up in a church in which this covenant was talked about, but I was never actually invited to enter into the covenant with God. I was told, "If you believe that Jesus was truly the Son of God and that He died for your sins, your sins will be forgiven, and you will go to heaven and not to hell after you die." Since I didn't want to go to hell after I died, I said, "OK, I believe those facts." However, what I never understood was that the issue was not "belief," but rather entering into covenant by giving up to God the authority to govern my life. I just continued to run my own life, do what I wanted, and "believed" in Jesus. (The Bible says that the demons believe that Jesus was the Son of God and died for the sins of all men. However, this belief does not mean that the demons have entered into covenant with God.)

When I went away to college, I was quite shocked when someone explained to me that believing that Yeshua had died for my sins did not make me a partaker in the New

Covenant. It was as though through all the years I had gone to church, people had told me that there was a ticket to America available and that I should believe that fact, which I did. However, no one ever asked me, "Would you actually like to buy this ticket and embark on the journey?"

Consequently, I suddenly realized in college that I had never yet bought the ticket, and had not yet even become a partaker of the New Covenant that God had made available to me by the blood of Messiah (Christ). When this realization came to me, I also understood that, like the Scotsman, I would have to trade my entire life thus far and authority over my future life for this covenant (ticket) with God. I weighed the cost and decided that I would be a fool not to do so. This turned out to be a defining moment in my life when everything changed. I entered into covenant and traded my entire life for the life of Yeshua living through me.

Perhaps you are just realizing right now that you have never entered into this New Covenant. Maybe you are like I was, saying, "Well, I believe in Jesus," or "I prayed the prayer to be born again." But in reality you have never entered into covenant, exchanging your entire life for the life of Yeshua. You are still running your own life, and begging God to help you when you are pressured or in trouble. I would be remiss if I did not offer you an opportunity to enter into the New Covenant right now and to exchange your life for the life of Messiah Yeshua (Christ Jesus). If you would like to enter into that covenant with God, or even to reaffirm the covenant you have already entered into, I invite you to pray out loud the following prayer. However, please don't pray this prayer if you are not serious about giving up the rest of your life to be and do whatever God wants for your life.

Father God, I desire today to receive Your offer of being grafted into Your New Covenant. I realize that entering into covenant with You means that I give up everything I have and everything I desire (my entire life) to You. In exchange, You will forgive my sin, remove my iniquity and empower me with Your authority and Your Holy Spirit. I further understand that a covenant requires unconditional surrender to You.

With this understanding, I today ask you to forgive me for withholding my life from You up until now. Please forgive me for all of my sin and iniquity. Today, I unconditionally surrender to You and exchange my life for the Life of Messiah Yeshua (Jesus Christ), Who died and gave up His life for me. I embrace Your offer of eternal life, and if I never did so before, today I "purchase the ticket" by giving You the rest of my life. I ask You to take my life, do whatever You want to with me, and make me the person You want me to be. God, I withhold nothing from You. I make myself Your servant from this day forth to do anything, go anywhere, and be anything that You desire of me.

Furthermore, a covenant will do you no good if you have entered into it but have never activated it. Many people think that by simply having a covenant with God they will be greatly benefited. No doubt that there is incredible value in having a covenant, but if you have never embraced or exercised any of the privileges or responsibilities of that covenant, then you will live life basically just like everyone else who has no covenant. Suppose that the Scotsman purchased the ticket but never used it. The ticket still has great value, but unless he goes to the pier and boards the ship, he will never arrive in America. Just having the ticket in and of itself is of very little practical value in terms of accomplishing the purpose for which the ticket was issued.

I have met some people who have truly entered into the New Covenant, but never understood the purpose of the covenant. They thought that somehow just having the covenant would protect them or benefit them, "Because I am a Christian...," or "Because I am born again, nothing bad will ever happen to me." However, just like simply having the ocean passage ticket will not get one to America, simply entering into and having a covenant with God will not in and of itself accomplish God's purpose in covenant. As noted above, one must also <u>know</u> the privileges and responsibilities of the covenant, and be willing to enforce such against enemies.

Bicycle Knowledge

What does it mean to <u>know</u> the covenants of promise? A person may have an intellectual knowledge of the Covenant, but not have an experiential, heart revelation knowledge of the covenant. Thus, one can "know" the covenant (intellectual) but not <u>know</u> (heart revelation) the covenant. Many people spend much time studying the Bible, but yet have very little heart revelation of the promises of covenant. They certainly don't have the inner heart confidence (I call it bicycle knowledge) to confront enemies or works of the enemy, expecting that the exercise of their covenant authority will release God's supernatural power.

Let me give you a couple of examples. Riding a bicycle is a good example that comes to mind. Suppose a very intelligent 30-year-old man reads an extensive book on the theory and practice of riding a bicycle. He could then truthfully state, "I know how to ride a bicycle." However, this man has never actually ridden a bicycle.

On the other hand, suppose we also have a 7-year-old boy who has never read a book on bicycles, but who rides a bike a couple hours every day. This boy can also state, "I know how to ride a bicycle." Now, if both of these people enter a three-kilometer bicycle race, which one of these two people would you expect to win the race? They both *know* how to ride a bicycle. However, for the man, the knowledge is only intellectual, while for the boy the knowledge is experiential heart knowledge. Of course, the boy would win the race. In reality, the man is still a stranger to the bicycle, while the boy is a partaker of true revelational bicycle knowledge. I have come to call this experiential type of revelational knowledge, "*bicycle knowledge.*"

Let me give you one other practical example. Which of the following two men would you rather engage to pilot an airplane in which you and your family will ride? A man who passed his private pilot written exam with a 100% score, but has never flown an airplane, or a man who only got a 70% on his private pilot written exam, but has flown commercially for several years and has accumulated 5,000 hours of flight experience? Again, both men could truthfully state, "I know how to fly an airplane."

> When pressure or crisis hits our lives, it is not what we intellectually know that can help us, but rather what we have ingrained as an image in our hearts.

Many people have read, studied, and even memorized the Bible, and can say, "I know the covenants of promise," but in reality, they do not know (revelational heart knowledge) and are in actuality still strangers to the covenants of promise. Unfortunately, when pressure or crisis hits our lives, it is not what we intellectually know that can help us, but rather what we have ingrained as an image in our hearts that helps us. In crisis, we respond out of the heart, not out of the mind.

What Am I Going To Do? vs. What Has God Said?

I have said for years that one can always tell if someone has bicycle knowledge or just intellectual knowledge of the covenant promises of God by just listening to his/her language when pressure of crisis hits his/her life. The person who <u>knows</u> the covenant asks, "What has God said?" The person who is a stranger to the covenant asks, "What am I going to do?" The first one asks, "What has God said?" because he understands that if he knows what God has said, he then knows what God will do. Why? The reason is because God is a covenant keeper and will always (100% of the time) do exactly what He said He would do. The one who is not a stranger to the covenant has developed an inner image that simply knows the faithfulness of God and relies upon Him to perform His word, while the stranger to the covenant may intellectually know the words, but does not have an inner image of God's faithfulness to perform His word.

Let's now look at an example in scripture. Both King Saul and David were called upon to respond to Goliath. What was the difference between these two men? They both served the same God. They both were circumcised into the same covenant. God loved them both the same. They both had the same opportunity to confront and kill Goliath. God's promise was the same to both of them. What was the difference? Why didn't Saul go kill Goliath? In the end, we will find that although both men were partakers of the same covenant with God, in reality Saul was a stranger to the covenants of promise and David was not.

Let's first of all look at God's covenant promise to Israel regarding this matter.

Hear, O Israel: you are to cross over the Jordan today, and go in to dispossess nations greater and mightier than yourself, cities great and fortified up to heaven, a people great and tall, the descendants of the Anakim, whom you know, and of whom you heard it said, 'Who can stand before the descendants of Anak?' Therefore understand today that the LORD your God is He who goes over before you as a consuming fire. <u>*He will destroy them and bring them down before you;*</u> *so you shall drive them out and destroy them quickly, as the LORD has said to you.* (Deuteronomy 9:1-3)

Here we see an incredible covenant promise given to Israel. God Almighty tells them that when they cross the Jordan River and come into the land, there they will meet the sons of Anak. Now who were the sons of Anak? These were the so-called giants in the land (Numbers 13:33; Deuteronomy 2:11). These were the same sons of Anak (giants) that the ten spies encountered in Numbers chapter eleven. In that encounter, eight of the spies were so badly frightened that they refused to go into the land. In this passage, God has said that Israel will again encounter these giant sons of Anak, but that they should not be afraid. God Himself, will go before them as a consuming fire and He will destroy these giants.

What is required of the sons of Israel when they encounter the giants? Their primary job is to show up and collect miracles as God fulfills His covenant promise to them. To whom was this promise made? It was made to any Israelite man in covenant with God. Since circumcision was the outward sign of covenant with God, this promise was for any circumcised Israelite.

Now, several generations later during the reign of King Saul, Israel once again encounters these giants, specifically one named Goliath of Gath. Several questions come to mind. Who would be the one you would think would go out to enforce God's covenant promise against this Philistine giant? Would you not think that it would be the King of Israel, Saul? Had Saul ever read God's promise in Deuteronomy chapter nine? Of course he had. He was a Hebrew man who probably memorized Deuteronomy. Did Saul know the promise of covenant? No doubt he did, intellectually. Did this promise do him any good whatsoever? Not really. Why not? The primary reason is because Saul was a stranger to the covenants of promise. He had read this promise and knew it in his mind, but he had no bicycle knowledge of this promise. It simply wasn't in his heart. So when confronted by the giant, rather than asking, "What has God said?" Saul asked, "What are we going to do? How can we find a warrior big enough and skilled enough to kill Goliath?"

David, no doubt, had also read this promise in Deuteronomy, chapter nine. However, he had specific bicycle knowledge of God's faithfulness to keep His covenant promises. How did David get this inner image of God's faithfulness? I believe that this happened through multiple challenges that David faced in the field while tending his father's sheep. He explains two of these experiences to King

Saul as recorded in 1 Samuel 17:34-37. Let me give you below the "Craig Hill amplified version" of David's experiences.

David spent most of his time in the fields looking after his father's sheep. I believe that He must have received a word from the Lord granting him God's authority to protect the sheep in his charge. The word was probably something like this: "David, if any wild beast threatens or attacks your father's sheep, I grant you authority in My name to attack and kill it. I will go before you as a consuming fire and destroy any such wild beasts."

That's a really great promise from God. The problem with most promises from God is that the only way the promise moves from intellectual ascent to heart (bicycle) knowledge is by testing out the promise in life experience. Sure enough, a couple weeks later a lion appeared in the clearing where David's sheep were grazing. As the lion moved toward the outer edges of the sheep, getting ready to pounce on one of them, David became aware of his presence and yelled at the lion. The lion, now losing interest in the sheep, stood upright and stared at David.

At this point, it became very evident to the 15-year-old shepherd that this lion was now preparing to attack him. He had to make a split second decision to run toward the lion, or run away from it. Suddenly, the word of God's promise came roaring out of his spirit into his mind. David realized that the stakes were very high. If he ran toward the lion and God did not supernaturally kill it, David had no natural chance to overcome a full-grown male lion, and the lion would swiftly kill him. David made his choice. He charged toward the lion.

David doesn't tell us what he was thinking as he ran toward that lion, but if he was like most of us, he was probably thinking, "I hope that thought really was from

God. I hope it wasn't just my wishful thinking. Or maybe it was a deception from the devil and I will get killed." However, when he reached the lion, as the lion roared and launched himself into the air toward David's throat, the young shepherd grabbed the lion by his mane under his throat, and with his other hand clubbed the lion with the large stick in his hand.

Actually, we are not told exactly how the lion was killed, but it is evident that God did something beyond David's natural ability. Below is David's own account to Saul of killing the lion.

But David said to Saul, "Your servant used to keep his father's sheep, and when a lion or a bear came and took a lamb out of the flock, I went out after it and struck it, and delivered the lamb from its mouth; and when it arose against me, I caught it by its beard, and struck and killed it." (1 Samuel 17:34-35)

Right after the boy and the lion fell to the ground, David shook himself off, stood and looked to survey what had just happened. There, motionless on the ground, was the ferocious lion, which only moments before had threatened to end David's life. I imagine that right about then an explosion erupted in this young shepherd's spirit.

"Alright! Awesome! Any more lions out there? Come on! Come on!"

At that moment, the knowledge of God's promise had moved from David's mind to an image preserved in his heart. It was no longer an untested theory, but rather a practical reality.

Another couple of weeks went by and a bear suddenly appeared in the meadow, again threatening David's sheep. This time, David didn't even think, but yelled and immediately ran toward the bear, confident that God would once again behave absolutely consistent with His word and would work through David to slay the bear. David was simply required to show up and exercise the authority that God had given him to release God's power to kill the bear. David grabbed the bear by the throat, thereby releasing God's power according to His promise, and the bear fell to the ground dead. Again, there was an explosion in David's spirit as his life experience confirmed to him the veracity of God's promises to him. While David had started out as a stranger to these promises, life experience had now tested the word of God, and he was no longer a stranger. He now had an image of God's word preserved in his heart.

Who Is This Uncircumcised Philistine?

One day some time later, David's father called to him and asked him to take some lunch up to his older brothers, who were in the camp of the Israelite army preparing to engage in battle with the Philistines. David agreed, happy in his heart to have a break from the sheep for a day, and go up to see what was happening on the battlefield. When he arrived, he began talking with his brothers as to what was happening. Just then, the Philistine giant, Goliath, came out and began to taunt and mock the armies of Israel. David inquired, "What is going on here?"

The men explained to David that the Philistine had proposed to settle the battle between the two nations by allowing one man from each camp to fight to the death. The losing nation would then become slaves to the winning nation.

Becoming a slave in that time was a very serious matter. If your nation became the slaves of another nation, you gave up all rights to everything. You no longer had any possessions or privileges. The people of the conquering nation could take your wives and daughters to be their wives, kill your husbands, and put your children to forced labor. So losing the battle and becoming a slave to the Philistines was a very unpleasant proposition for the Israelites.

When David understood what Goliath had proposed, he was quite indignant, and questioned why no one had gone out to kill this giant. The men around him responded, "David, have you seen this giant? He is 10 feet tall, and has a spear like a weavers beam." Even David's own older brother mocked him.

However, the young shepherd responded with, "Who is this uncircumcised Philistine, that he should defy the armies of the living God?" (1 Samuel 17:26) David continued to use this word "uncircumcised" several times as an adjective to describe Goliath. Why? I believe that David was very aware that circumcision was a sign of the covenant with Yahweh (The LORD), the God of Heaven and Earth, and by using this word, "uncircumcised," David was continually reminding the others that this giant, Goliath, was a mere man fighting in human strength with no covenant authority or power from God. Any circumcised Israelite, on the other hand, was not a mere man fighting in human strength, but rather a covenant representative of God Almighty. His authority and power would thus be God's, not his own.

David seemed almost flippant about Goliath. It was as if he were saying, "Any circumcised Israelite could kill this uncircumcised clown. It is not dependent upon finding a big, strong, or experienced man. It is dependent upon finding a man who truly understands how to release the power of God by the authority he has been granted through the covenant, outwardly symbolized by circumcision. Even a child could do this. As a matter of fact, if no one else will do so, I'll be happy to go kill him. Would you like me to do this before lunch or after? By the way, is there a reward?"

Apparently, no one else in the camp of Israel had bicycle knowledge of what had been promised to the circumcised covenant man. Quickly, news of David's bold speech reached the ears of King Saul, who immediately sent for David. I wish we had a more detailed account available to us of the conversation in the tent that day between David and Saul. We only have available a record of a few sentences of the conversation. However, whatever David said to the king was so impressive that King Saul decided that this young, inexperienced shepherd had the best chance of any warrior in Israel of actually killing the giant. I really believe that the miracle that day was not that David killed Goliath, but rather that King Saul let him try.

Can you imagine if you were the king of Israel? You would be responsible for the lives of all of the families of Israel. The fate of every family was to be placed into the hands of one man who would be sent by the king to fight the Philistine giant. If the Israelite warrior lost, the entire nation would be subject to slavery at the cruel hands of the Philistines. You only get one chance, with one man. So whom would you send? Based on the conversation in the tent that day, King Saul decided to place the fate of every family in the entire nation in young David's hands. Now, this would be totally illogical in view of the fact that David was young, small, inexperienced and untrained.

In the brief record of the conversation, David explained to the king that he did have experience in battle in the sheep field by killing a lion and a bear. He then stated,

"Your servant has killed both lion and bear; and this uncircumcised Philistine will be like one of them, seeing he has defied the armies of the living God." Moreover David said, "The LORD, who delivered me from the paw of the lion and from the paw of the bear, He will deliver me from the hand of this Philistine." (1 Samuel 17:36-37)

King Saul decided that David was the man to kill the Philistine. Can you imagine what it must have been like in the camp of Israel that day? News began to go out that the King had found the champion of Israel who would defeat the Philistine giant and save them from slavery. One soldier told his friend, "Oh, our king is a great and wise man. I'll bet that he has found an experienced warrior 12 feet tall!"

"Yes," exclaimed his friend, "probably our champion can kill ten giants with one swipe of his sword!"

Soon news went out that the new champion of Israel was about to emerge from the king's tent and go to slay the giant. All eyes were upon the entrance to the king's tent. The tent flaps began to rustle as the hero was about to step out into sight. Finally, the tent flaps parted, and out stepped... a teenager–unarmed, no shield or protective mail, sporting the latest fashion in shepherds' robes, holding a sling shot and a couple of stones.

Can you imagine what the seasoned soldiers must have thought? "The fate of my wife and children is in his hands? Has the king gone mad? Whether my young daughter is tortured, violated, or killed by cruel Philistine soldiers or not is dependent upon this boy winning the battle? I don't think so!"

Today there would have been a congressional investigation and impeachment proceedings. That is why I say the miracle is not the defeat of Goliath, but rather that Israel allowed young David to represent the nation in the battle with the Philistine.

Amazingly enough, commissioned by King Saul, David went out to face the Philistine giant in his boyish shepherd's clothes, armed only with a slingshot and a few stones. The sight of this young unarmed Israelite coming to face Goliath infuriated the Philistine, as he was looking for a legitimate opponent to conquer. This appeared to him to be no contest at all. So he spat at David and said something like the following:

"What is this? Do you really think that you can fight with me, sonny boy? No armor? No weapons? You come with sticks and stones? Do I look like a scared little dog, sonny, that will run away if you hit me with a stick or throw a rock at me? What kind of an idiot do you have for a king, who would send a little boy out to fight with me? OK, if that's how you want it, come on. I'll squash you like a bug, and then feed you to the vultures and the wild beasts of the field. Come on!"

Then David said to the Philistine, "You come to me with a sword, with a spear, and with a javelin. But I come to you in the name of the LORD of hosts, the God of the armies of Israel, whom you have defied. This day the LORD will deliver you into my hand, and I will strike you and take your head from you. And this day I will give the carcasses of the camp of the Philistines to the birds of the air and the wild beasts of the earth, that all the earth may know that there is a God in Israel. Then all this assembly shall know that the LORD does not save with sword and spear; for the battle is the LORD's, and He will give you into our hands." (1 Samuel 17:45-47)

David truly understood that the issue here was not power, training, experience or weaponry, but rather <u>authority</u>. Covenant grants authority to release <u>God's power</u>. King Saul was literally a stranger to the covenant, even though he was a legitimate partaker in the covenant. The authority to release God's power according to God's promise in His Torah (Word) did not help Saul one bit because He didn't <u>know</u> (bicycle knowledge) the covenant, although he thought he knew (intellectual knowledge) it. Thus Saul's thought had been, "What are we going to do? We need to find a man who is larger, stronger and more experienced in battle than Goliath."

David, who had allowed God to implant within him a heart revelation of the covenant through life experience, was not a stranger to the covenant. His thought was totally different than King Saul's. David's thought was, "What has God said? If I know what God has said, then I know what God will do. I also know that my responsibility is not to provide the knowledge or the power, but rather to simply show up and use my covenant authority to release God's knowledge and power. I don't know exactly how God will kill the giant. I just know that He will because of the experience I have already had with the lion and the bear in the sheep field."

You probably are already well aware of the outcome of the battle. David did indeed sling a stone at the giant that struck him in the forehead and he fell to the ground. David then ran to him and cut off the giant Philistine's head with his own sword. I imagine that there was an explosion of renewed confidence and victory in David's spirit as he stood over Goliath and raised the bloody, decapitated head of the giant for all to see. Once again, his heart was filled with confidence of God's absolute faithfulness to fulfill His covenant promises. David had again proven to himself that his responsibility was to simply show up and exercise the authority given to him by God in covenant. Again, he discovered that if he would do so, God would do exactly what he said He would do in His word. Thus, David and all Israel saw before their very eyes that day the practical outworking of God's promise to them as recorded in Deuteronomy 9:1-3. The bottom line difference between David and Saul in the matter of confronting Goliath was that Saul was a stranger to the covenant promise in Deuteronomy chapter nine, and David was not.

I believe that it was God who killed the giant. Truly, I believe that David could have spit at the giant and it would have killed him. David's job was simply to show up, proclaim the policy of the Kingdom of God, and watch God release His power to enforce His Kingdom policy. God used the stone David slung at the giant, but he could have used anything. It wasn't David's job to figure out how to kill Goliath, but rather to proclaim God's Kingdom authority and trust God to provide the wisdom and power to enforce the policy.

If David had not previously run toward the lion and tested His covenant with God when the opportunity arose, he would not have been able to face the bear without running away. Had he not developed in the shepherd's field the confidence in God's faithfulness to do exactly what He had said He would, David would not have had the confidence to confront the Philistine giant with his covenant authority, expecting God to kill Goliath the same way He had the lion and the bear. Since neither Saul nor anyone else in Israel had confidence in the covenant promise of God, had David not shown up, Israel would have most likely been defeated by the Philistines. Undoubtedly, some well meaning believer would then have said, "Well, God is in control. So I guess that He wanted to teach us humility and servanthood through subjecting us to slavery to the Philistines."

Thus, we see that in the areas of life in which we are strangers to the covenant promises of God, we are in a sense between a rock and hard place. If we have run away from the opportunities that life has offered us to test the covenant promises of God when the stakes are not as high, we will then find ourselves like King Saul, being strangers to the covenant into which we have been grafted when the stakes are very high. King Saul, being a stranger to the covenant between Yahweh and Israel, was not able to confront Goliath with confident authority in God's covenant as he should have. If anyone in the camp of Israel should have confronted the Philistine enemy with the authority of covenant, it should have been the king. However, Saul had not "run toward the lion" as David had when the stakes were lower. So he had no true bicycle knowledge of the covenant promises.

Thus, if Saul would have said to the giant the things that David said without the inner confidence in God to fulfill His covenant word, Goliath would have had him for lunch. Attempting to pretend that you have bicycle knowledge when you really don't is always a disaster. This would be similar to pretending that you are confident in riding a bicycle when you have actually never ridden one before, but have only read a book about it. You will fall for sure and expose your ineptitude.

One of the most foolish things you can do is to try to fake bicycle knowledge when you really don't have it (e.g. flying a plane or riding a bike). Another example would be riding a horse. An experienced horsewoman with confidence can get on a spirited horse, and within seconds the horse knows who is boss and will obey. On the other hand, if an inexperienced woman mounts the same horse and uses a loud, strong, authoritative voice to try to convey confidence and authority, but actually lacks the inner confidence, that horse will perceive this also in seconds and will take that rider for a ride. One can't fake true inner confidence. A horse, a mean dog, a child, or even a demon can perceive actual inner confidence and authority almost immediately, and will behave accordingly (e.g. The seven sons of Sceva: Acts 19:13-16). Voice volume or intonation won't make up for lack of true inner authority.

Thus if, like King Saul, you are still a stranger to the covenant promises of God when the crisis or the enemy comes, you are truly between a rock and hard place. You can't exercise the authority of covenant because the bicycle knowledge is not really in your heart. You know it, and the enemy knows it. The best you can do is try to find a big, strong warrior, as King Saul was hoping to do, who can beat the giant by natural means. Or, even better yet, find someone who does have bicycle knowledge of the covenant like David, and engage that person's help as King Saul finally did.

Furthermore, if one does not understand that life is a moment-by-moment covenant relationship and partnership between God and man, one will fall into either of the two ditches on the sides of the road of truth. If one holds the belief that God is in control, and therefore God is the author of all circumstances, then one will not learn to test and come into bicycle knowledge of the covenant authority in which we are called to walk. One then remains a stranger to the covenants of promise and experiences many defeats at the hands of the enemy, which are then ascribed to God. Since He is in control, the thinking goes, He must want to teach us something or build character through devastation and defeat.

On the other hand, one can fall into the ditch of believing that victory is dependent totally upon my learning and implementing principles or authority from the word of God, independent of moment-by-moment relationship with God. Then, without God's knowledge and instruction, one attempts to implement principles and authority independently and again is defeated.

> Life is a covenant relationship and partnership that must be walked out in moment-by-moment intimacy and communication with the LORD.

This potentially leads to discouragement or to the conclusion that "God's word doesn't work" or that "He is not faithful."

The truth is that life is not all dependent upon God or all dependent upon me. Life is a covenant relationship and partnership that must be walked out in moment-by-moment intimacy and communication with the LORD.

Reflection

1. Many people are strangers from God's covenant and don't know it. Having a covenant in and of itself is only the first part toward implementation of the provisions of that covenant.

2. In order for a covenant to help you, three things must be true.

   a. You must receive the covenant and be an active partaker in it.

   b. You must know the privileges and responsibilities of the covenant.

   c. You must be willing to enforce the terms of the covenant against enemies.

3. Intellectual knowledge alone is not enough to defeat enemies. One must have "bicycle knowledge," or experiential heart revelation of the covenant.

4. King Saul possessed only intellectual knowledge of God's covenant toward Israel, while David possessed true heart revelation knowledge and used it to kill the Philistine giant.

5. In the circumstances of your life, have you behaved more as David or as Saul when confronted with the giants of adversity?

6. In what areas of your life do you truly have heart revelation "bicycle knowledge" of God's New Covenant, and in what areas are you still a stranger to the covenants of promise?

Resources

🎧 Ambassador or Tourist? (Single CD Teaching)

chapter 7
AMBASSADOR OR
TOURIST?

In the last chapter we talked about the fact that many times we find ourselves as partakers of the New Covenant, but are in reality strangers to it. However, it is not only the promises from which we are strangers, but also the representative responsibilities of covenant. An eastern man understands that when he enters into covenant, he becomes a representative, or an ambassador, as it were, of the one with whom he has made covenant. Thus, when we were grafted into the New Covenant, we became ambassadors of the Kingdom of Heaven. We are no longer private citizens, but rather we are representatives of a Kingdom and a King.

Have you ever really thought through the reason why after you were grafted into the New Covenant and gave your life to Messiah, you were not simply taken immediately to heaven? I have thought a lot about this. Why did He leave you here on an earth filled with evil, injustice, sickness, etc.? There are probably many reasons, but your personal happiness and pleasure would for sure not be one of them. If the goal of life is to be happy, then God should not have left you on a demon-infested planet full of unjust sinners. He should have taken you to heaven immediately.

Sometimes I have asked parents what is their deepest desire for their children. Many have responded by saying, "I just want my children to be happy." I have always thought to respond by saying, "Then the best thing that could happen would be for your children to die and go to heaven today. Because in heaven there is no injustice or evil, no mean people, no death, no sickness, and no sorrow. But here on earth we experience a lot of death, sickness, sorrow, evil and injustice."

The main point is that we are not left on the planet after we have entered into covenant with God to be happy, or to serve and please ourselves. God has left us here to be His Kingdom ambassadors and to partner with Him by using our authority to implement Kingdom policy and release His power, His rule and His reign here upon the earth. We are not here to have a nice life, make as much money as we can, or have as much fun as we can. We are not left here to please ourselves and do what we want. We are here to serve at the pleasure of the King. It is our job to partner with Him in relationship, to draw others into His Kingdom, and as His ambassadors, to implement His policies here on earth.

When we entered into the New Covenant with Yahweh (the LORD), it was as if we had joined the army of a nation. Joining the army causes a man to cease to be a private citizen, and become an actual representative of the government of that nation. Imagine how ridiculous it might be for someone to join the army, but never really understand the concept that he is no longer a private citizen. Such a person would not be able to make any sense out of the circumstances of life. Suppose that this person became a part of the U.S. Army during World War II, and was then taken into the war zone in Europe.

What if this soldier was still thinking as a private citizen, yet was wearing a military uniform? He would not be able to understand why the German soldiers were so unfriendly and were actually trying to kill him. Such a person might say, "What have I done to deserve this treatment? I have never done anything to them. Why are they so antagonistic?" Such a person would not understand that the issue is not personal and does not depend upon his personal behavior or attitudes, but rather is only due to the fact that he represents a government that is at war with Germany.

I have found that many people have not understood that when they entered into the New Covenant with God, just like the soldier described above, they actually became representatives of God on a planet that is still part of a war zone. Part of the exchange that takes place when we become partakers of the New Covenant is that of ambassadorial representation. Yeshua becomes your ambassador in Heaven before the Father. Likewise, you have become Yeshua's ambassador here on earth representing His Kingdom. This is what He told His followers.

So Jesus (Yeshua) said to them again, "Peace to you! As the Father has sent Me, I also send you." (John 20:21)

This above statement is a commissioning by Yeshua of his disciples as ambassadors.

Apostle Paul further tells us directly that we have become ambassadors of the LORD when we were grafted into the New Covenant.

...that is, that God was in Christ reconciling the world to Himself, not imputing their trespasses to them, and has committed to us the word of reconciliation. Now then, <u>we are ambassadors for Christ,</u> as though God were pleading through us: we implore you on Christ's behalf, be reconciled to God. (2 Corinthians 5:19-20)

So we, who are partakers of the New Covenant, have become ambassadors of the One with Whom we are in covenant. We talked in the last chapter about promises that are available to us by covenant. In this chapter, we are now talking also about responsibilities that go along with being an ambassador of the Kingdom of God.

> So we, who are partakers of the New Covenant, have become ambassadors of the One with Whom we are in covenant.

Even though we actually are ambassadors, I have found that most believers still think and function on the earth as if they were private citizens, or tourists. So the question arises: Are you living your life as an ambassador or as a tourist? There would be quite a difference.

Just to be clear, let me contrast below some of the responsibilities and privileges of an ambassador with those of a tourist.

Ambassador	Tourist
• Speaks words in the name of the government he represents	• Speaks his own personal words in his own name
• Conveys no personal opinion, but only the policies of his government	• Conveys his own personal opinions
• His words are backed up by the treasury and military might of His nation	• His words are backed up by his own personal bank account and strength
• Is concerned only with the interests of the government he represents	• Is concerned only with his own personal interests
• Maintains connection and communication with his government headquarters	• Maintains no connection with his government headquarters
• Carries out the policies of his government	• Carries out his own personal policies
• Spends his priority time carrying out the assignments of his government	• Spends his priority time pleasing himself and doing as he wishes
• His government provides transportation, housing, food, clothing, security and meets all of his personal needs	• He must provide his own transportation, housing, food, clothing, security and meet all of his own personal needs

When the President of the United States wants to communicate something with a foreign government he does not usually travel to that foreign country himself. Normally, he communicates through his ambassador. Imagine what it would be like if the United States government sent a person as an ambassador overseas to the nation of France, for example, but this man never understood or received his

131

commission as an ambassador. Somehow, he just thought that the U.S. government had sent him and his family on an all-expense-paid trip to Paris, France as tourists. As a result of this misunderstanding, he may never check his e-mail, fax, or phone messages. He never checks in with Washington to find out what his assignments might be or what messages he is to deliver to the French president.

When Washington is attempting to find him to deliver an important message to the French government, the U.S. ambassador can't be found because he is out sightseeing with his family and is at that moment enjoying the view of Paris from the top of the Eiffel Tower. Such an ambassador, who is behaving as a private citizen, is of very little use to the government that dispatched him!

I believe that many times this is the frustration of heaven. Many of the ambassadors never check in with headquarters to see if there is a message that needs to be delivered to someone, or a policy that needs to be explained or enforced. We understand that an ambassador is also a private citizen. If he speaks a word on behalf of his government in his role as ambassador, that word is backed up by the government that sent him. However, if he speaks the same word as a tourist, or a private citizen, not in his capacity as an ambassador, that word means nothing. I believe that many times if an ambassador does not understand his role as an ambassador but only perceives himself as a private citizen, it strips him of any confidence to speak a word from the King, expecting that the King and His government will back up that word.

In considering our New Covenant commission as ambassadors of the Kingdom of God, it is also important to understand the scope of our ambassadorship. You may be thinking, "Alright, I understand and accept the fact that I am an ambassador, but to whom and in what context?" I believe that there are various scopes of ambassadorship that God has given to us as His representatives. Some of us may find ourselves as ambassadors to a nation, others to a city, still others to a business or school. Every New Covenant representative is at least an ambassador to a family and sphere of influence.

In the mid 1980s, I had the privilege of becoming acquainted with a Nigerian man, the late Dr. Benson Idahosa, who really had a better understanding of his Kingdom commission as an ambassador than almost anyone I have ever met. Dr. Idahosa had come to realize in the early years of walking with the LORD that he was not left on planet earth as a private citizen, here to please himself. He realized, rather, that he was here as a Kingdom ambassador, to serve at the pleasure of the King. As I understand it, when Dr. Idahosa first began to proclaim the gospel in the 1970s, there were still human sacrifices being offered on the streets of his city, Benin City, Nigeria. There were only a few thousand New Covenant believers in the entire city of over 1.2 million inhabitants. By the late 1980s, thanks to the ministry of Dr. Idahosa, I was told that there were over eight hundred thousand believers.

In the early days of his ministry, Dr. Idahosa had many people in his city threaten his life. He was told that they would kill him if he continued to preach the gospel and bring people into covenant with God. Because of all the death threats, Dr. Idahosa was forced to learn at a very early time in his walk with God that he was an ambassador of the Kingdom of God and that he did not need to try to protect his own life. He quickly learned that ambassadors enjoy the security and protection of the government they serve. He quickly had many testimonies of the supernatural power of

God and angels protecting his life as evil people had tried to kill him.

As time progressed, Dr. Idahosa's ministry impacted the entire nation of Nigeria and began to impact people in other nations as well. It became very evident that God had given him a commission as an ambassador from the Kingdom of God to the nation of Nigeria. So his scope of ambassadorship had extended beyond his family, church, and city, to his nation.

I Cancel the Witchcraft Conference

One of the best examples of this understanding of being an ambassador from Heaven rather than a private citizen is illustrated in the following testimony that the late Dr. Idahosa shared with me in the mid 1980s, at a time I was visiting him and his ministry in Nigeria. I will recount the story, as I recall the details that Dr. Idahosa shared with me.

At this time, Dr. Idahosa had a regular national television broadcast in Nigeria. It had come to his attention that the chief proponent of witchcraft in the country had scheduled an international witchcraft conference in Benin City. Ten thousand witches from around the world were registered for the conference that was to be held in a couple of month's time. During a time of preaching on the television program, Dr. Idahosa heard the Holy Spirit say to him to cancel the upcoming witchcraft conference.

Now, this type of statement is definitely not something that a private citizen could or would do. Rather, this is a declaration of policy that a governmental ambassador might pronounce. Having received a communiqué from head-quarters, Dr. Idahosa boldly proclaimed on Nigerian national television that the upcoming witchcraft conference in Benin

City would not take place. He declared that as of this day, he was canceling the conference.

Shortly after the broadcast, Dr. Idahosa flew out of the country on a ministry trip abroad. When he returned home, the press met him at the airport. Meanwhile, the chief witch who had convened the conference was up in arms about Dr. Idahosa's statement. The press agents advised Dr. Idahosa that the chief witch had gone on national television himself and denounced Dr. Idahosa.

"Who does he think he is?" the man had retorted. "Idahosa cannot cancel our witchcraft conference. Ten thousand people from around the world have already registered. All the flights have been booked. The venue is booked. The hotel reservations have all been made. Idahosa cannot stop this conference. As a matter of fact," he glowered, "even God Himself will not stop this conference!"

The press agents, after reporting this to Dr. Idahosa at the airport upon his return to the country, then asked, "So what do you say about that?"

Dr. Idahosa responded by saying, "I agree with the man."

"You do?" they queried. "How can you agree with him?"

Dr. Idahosa then looked straight into the camera and stated something like the following, "I agree with the man that God will not stop this conference." He then continued, "God will not waste His time to come to a city where He has sent His ambassador. **In the Name of Jesus, I cancel the conference**!"

Now there is a man who understands that he is not a private citizen or tourist, but rather is an ambassador of the Kingdom of God! He was not proclaiming his own word, some wishful thinking, or a "faith statement." He was simply delivering the message that he had heard from his government headquarters, and then relying upon his King and His government to back up the word.

Not understanding our role as ambassador, many of us faced with the same situation might have simply prayed, "Lord, please stop the witchcraft conference in our city." We would be asking God to do what He has dispatched us to do. Now I am not suggesting that we are to make presumptuous proclamations "in His name" without His authorization. However, I think that many times we are crying out to God and begging Him to do what He has dispatched us to do. We are then confused and feel rejected when our prayers "are not answered" or "nothing happens."

Had David not shown up on the battlefield, King Saul might have waited forever for God to do something about the giant, and then when Israel was eventually defeated by the Philistines, he would have felt abandoned and forsaken by God. Dr. Idahosa could have prayed for God to stop the witchcraft conference, and then felt that God had not "answered" his prayer when the conference continued anyway. This is how tourists think and behave. An ambassador is constantly checking in with headquarters and asking the question of the King, "What would You like me to say or do as Your ambassador within my sphere of influence today?"

> I think that many times we are crying out to God and begging Him to do what He has dispatched us to do.

Continuing on with the story, Dr. Idahosa did confess to me privately when he was recounting to me the story a few years later, that after he spoke these words, he did ask the LORD how He was planning to terminate the witchcraft conference. He didn't receive an immediate answer, but did have a calm assurance that he had heard correctly and had delivered the correct policy edict from his King.

About two days later, a lawyer in one of Dr. Idahosa's congregations asked for an appointment with him and advised him of a very interesting, but little-known point of law. The lawyer told him that he had been doing some study in the law books recently and had run across a federal law that was still on the books making the practice of witchcraft a federal offense, punishable by death. He had discovered that witchcraft was actually a capital crime in Nigeria at that time. The lawyer further stated that the law was not well known and almost impossible to enforce because of the predominance of Juju occult practices and other forms of witchcraft practiced all over the country, but especially in the rural areas.

Dr. Idahosa asked to see a copy of that law. The attorney was happy to provide him with the reference and a copy of the citation of the law. Meanwhile, the chief witch, still infuriated over the bold statements that Dr. Idahosa had made, had challenged him to a public debate on national television only a week or two before the conference was to be held. Dr. Idahosa accepted the invitation. When the evening of the debate arrived, Dr. Idahosa was ready with the copy of the federal law in hand.

The chief witch spoke first and went on for about forty-five minutes. After his conclusion, Dr. Idahosa announced, "My talk will be very short. I only have one question for the gentleman." He then asked, "Sir, please tell us, are you personally a practitioner of witchcraft? And if you are, I have power to kill you! Please tell us."

The man, knowing himself of the existence of the law, quickly stated, "No I do not personally practice witchcraft."

Dr. Idahosa then concluded, "That is what I thought." He then cited the federal law making witchcraft a capital offense in the country of Nigeria, after which he proclaimed something like, "Once again, in the Name of Jesus, I cancel the witchcraft conference. And I furthermore call upon the president of our nation to cancel all of the visas granted to the foreign guests, who are all practitioners of witchcraft, planning to attend this conference. In doing so, Mr. President, you would spare our country the embarrassment of having to arrest and put to death nearly ten thousand foreign tourists coming here to commit a capital offense."

With that, Dr. Idahosa concluded his remarks and finished the broadcast. Only moments after they were off the air, the telephone at the television station was ringing. It was someone from the office of the President wanting to have the exact citation of the law that Dr. Idahosa had quoted. Apparently after reviewing the law, the President was also very concerned about the ramifications of the witchcraft conference as pertaining to the law. Consequently, very shortly thereafter his office did indeed cancel all of the visas granted to the foreign visitors planning to attend the conference. This resulted in the cancellation of the conference due to lack of funding to carry it out and the threat of potential arrest and execution.

The point of this testimony is that the word of an ordinary private citizen canceling a conference would not mean much. However, when one is an ambassador of the King, who understands his ambassadorship and is accustomed to checking in with the King for communiqués and instructions, issues a proclamation or edict, we see that it is indeed enforced by the King himself. The ambassador is not usually called upon to provide the force to back up his government's policy. That is the job of the King, His government, and military. The job of the ambassador is to show up, speak forth the word of the King, and release the authority of the government to act in wisdom and power.

Thus, Dr. Idahosa's job was not to figure out how to stop the witchcraft conference. His job was only to proclaim the policy of the Kingdom and his King. It was the job of the King (the LORD) to provide the wisdom and power to terminate the conference.

In the previous chapter, we looked at the scriptural event of the confrontation between the armies of Israel and the Philistine giant, Goliath. We saw that the primary difference between Saul and David was their understanding of covenant ambassadorship. David understood that he was an ambassador of Yahweh, the God of Israel, while Saul only understood that he was an ambassador of the nation of Israel, but not the God of Israel.

Consequently, Saul thought that it was his job to figure out how to kill the giant, while David understood that by covenant he represented the authority of God, not just the authority of the nation of Israel. Therefore, he understood that it was God's job to provide the power to kill the giant. David's job was to show up and proclaim the policy of God and to use the authority delegated to him by God to release the government of Heaven to act to enforce that policy. So in reality, in terms of the government of Yahweh, the God of Heaven, Saul perceived himself only as a private citizen, or a tourist, as it were, while David perceived himself as a Kingdom ambassador of Yahweh, sent to proclaim the terms and policy of his government.

I Will Never Again Flood the Earth

I believe that because we have not understood and have been strangers from covenant, many times we have not understood how to interpret life's circumstances. Covenant really is the key to understanding how God operates on the earth. God will always act according to His character and His covenant Word. I believe that Satan relentlessly tries to make it look as though God acts randomly on the earth; as though it is a mystery as to how God will act or respond. For many people, it seems that God is like a dysfunctional, alcoholic father, who is kind one day, and mercilessly beats you the next day for doing the exact same thing. Some people's perception is that God speaks to their boss at work to give them a huge raise one day, and the next day gives their husband cancer.

You will even hear people say things such as, "You just never know what God is going to do. God acts in strange and mysterious ways." No, He doesn't! This is nonsense. God does exactly what He said He would do in His covenant word. The primary problem is that we have not known God's covenant promises; we have not understood that He will always keep His word and do exactly what He said He would do. This lack of understanding then causes incredible confusion in the interpretation of life experiences.

Let me give you an example of the difficulty someone might have if they don't know or understand covenant. Suppose you heard that because of global warming, the polar ice caps were rapidly melting and within a few months most of the entire earth's continental masses were going to be flooded with water in a global type flood. Perhaps you would hear some Bible teachers now proclaiming that this was

God's judgment upon the world because of the increase of sin. How would you know how to interpret this event?

Let me say very simply that if you understand covenant and God's faithfulness to His own word, you would immediately know that this event of a global flood could not be of God at all, and that it should be resisted, not accepted. How would you know this? You would know it from remembering and understanding the covenant that God made with humanity at the time of Noah. Let's look at this covenant promise.

Then God spoke to Noah and to his sons with him, saying: "And as for Me, behold, I establish My covenant with you and with your descendants after you, and with every living creature that is with you: the birds, the cattle, and every beast of the earth with you, of all that go out of the ark, every beast of the earth. Thus I establish My covenant with you: Never again shall all flesh be cut off by the waters of the flood; never again shall there be a flood to destroy the earth." And God said: "This is the sign of the covenant which I make between Me and you, and every living creature that is with you, for perpetual generations: I set My rainbow in the cloud, and it shall be for the sign of the covenant between Me and the earth. It shall be, when I bring a cloud over the earth, that the rainbow shall be seen in the cloud; and I will remember My covenant which is between Me and you and every living creature of all flesh; the waters shall never again become a flood to destroy all flesh. The rainbow shall be in the cloud, and I will look on it to remember the everlasting covenant between God and every living creature of all flesh that is on the earth." And God said to Noah, "This is the sign of the covenant which I have established between Me and all flesh that is on the earth." (Genesis 9:8-17)

We see here that God clearly stated He would never flood the earth again. So if we hear that there is a global flood coming, we would categorically know that this is not the judgment of God for one simple reason. He made a covenant stating that He would never flood the earth again. How would I interpret such a circumstance? I would know that it is not from God. It is either emanating from the foolishness of man or from the kingdom of darkness. Therefore, as an ambassador, I would want to check in with the King to find out how He wants me to respond to this event that is not coming from Him. But because of this covenant word, I would not spend one minute questioning whether this was God's judgment or not.

Now, let's look at another covenant promise recorded in Isaiah 54 that relates back to this covenant. Isaiah 54 is written to those who have entered into the New Covenant, inaugurated by the blood of Messiah spoken of in Isaiah 53. In verses nine and ten, God speaks the following to those of us grafted into this New Covenant:

"For this is like the waters of Noah to Me; For as I have sworn That the waters of Noah would no longer cover the earth, So have I sworn That I would not be angry with you, nor rebuke you. For the mountains shall depart, And the hills be

removed, But My kindness shall not depart from you, Nor shall My covenant of peace be removed," Says the LORD, *who has mercy on you.* (Isaiah 54:9-10)

In this passage above, Yahweh has said that He has made a covenant of peace, with those who have received His New Covenant, which is certain and shall never be removed. He further states that the promises of this covenant are as certain as the fact that the earth will never again be flooded. What does this mean in practical reality? It means that God is not random; forgiving you one day, but punishing you for your sin the next. The reason I say this is because this is actually how some people think of God. They cannot distinguish between the works of God and the works of Satan, which Yeshua came to destroy (1 John 3:8).

The Divine Exchange of Covenant

So if you have been grafted into the New Covenant by the blood of Messiah Yeshua, then your sin has been forgiven and your iniquity has been laid upon Him. A divine exchange has taken place. When you entered into the covenant, Yeshua took your sin and iniquity, and you took His righteousness. Let me state the obvious. When you make an exchange, it is like a sales transaction. If you walk into a store, give the clerk $15 in exchange for a CD, she keeps the money, and you keep the CD. It is an exchange. You can't keep the $15 and the CD; the clerk can't keep the CD and the $15. You walk in with $15 and no CD. You walk out with the CD and no $15.

I remember praying one time for a woman in one of our seminars who had been conceived out of wedlock in an

143

evening of passion between her mother and a man she didn't love, who never married her. This daughter had never met her natural father, but revealed to us that she had always carried on the inside, a feeling of being "illegitimate," "not wanted," and "a mistake." As I asked the LORD how He wanted to minister to her, I heard Him say, *"Tell her that all My life on earth I was thought to have been of illegitimate birth. No one but My mother and father, Joseph, really understood what had taken place at My birth. Consequently, everyone thought that I was conceived in fornication, and I wore that hideous name, 'bastard,' all the days of my earthly life.*

"Tell her that I never once disputed or rebutted being called by that name, even though it wasn't true. Please tell her that I received upon Myself those names, 'bastard, illegitimate, and mistake,' all of My earthly life on her behalf. She has entered into covenant with Me, but she has never let me take what I purchased from her. She took My righteousness and kept her shame. This is not an exchange. Please tell her that if she is now willing, I would like to experientially, in her heart, take her shame of 'bastard, illegitimate, and mistake' and exchange those feelings for those which I purchased for her by My blood of 'beloved, accepted, highly valued, planned for and wanted.' Please ask her to let Me implement the exchange that I wanted her to make when she first made covenant with Me."

When I shared these words of Yeshua with this daughter, she broke down and wept profusely as she realized that she had been holding onto what the LORD had actually died to purchase from her with His blood. She then asked Him to make that exchange with her that evening. It was then evident to us that she was having a powerful spiritual experience with the resurrected, living Messiah Yeshua. She later reported to us that when she asked Him to make that exchange, she literally felt Him remove from her a cloak of shame and illegitimacy she had worn all of her life. He then wrapped around her His own royal garment of honor. The feelings in her heart were experientially changed that evening, such that she could not make herself feel unwanted, illegitimate, or like a mistake, even if she tried. Those feelings were simply gone in the covenant exchange with Yeshua. This had not happened before because the young woman simply did not know that this had already been done for her by covenant. She had taken the CD, as it were, and yet refused to let Yeshua have the $15.

I have found that many people don't understand this regarding sickness and disease. Some, not understanding covenant exchange, believe that God is judging them with sickness due to some sin or fault on their part. However, if God placed your disease upon Messiah Yeshua in exchange for His health, then how could He justly put that disease back upon you when Yeshua has taken it in exchange? This would not be an exchange if you keep what you had. Again, when you walk into the store and exchange the $15 for the CD, you will never again have that $15. You now instead have the CD that was exchanged for the $15. This exchange regarding sin, iniquity, grief, sorrow and disease is spoken of in the provisions of the New Covenant described in Isaiah 53.

He is despised and rejected by men, a Man of sorrows and acquainted with grief. And we hid, as it were, our faces from Him; He was despised, and we did not esteem Him. Surely He has borne our griefs, and carried our sorrows; Yet we esteemed Him stricken, smitten by God, and afflicted. But He was wounded for our transgressions, He was bruised for our iniquities; The chastisement for our peace was upon Him, and by His stripes we are healed. All we like sheep have gone astray; we have turned, every one, to his own way; and the LORD has laid on Him the iniquity of us all. (Isaiah 53:3-6)

One peculiar thing I have sometimes run into is that people who are strangers from the covenants of promise and believe that God has placed a disease upon someone's life to build character or "to get their attention," will none the less still take that sick loved one to the doctor. They will then relentlessly make the sick person take medication, or subject him to surgery. I have often wanted to ask, "If you really believe that this sickness is from God, why on earth would you take your loved one to the doctor?" That rascal will try to make the sick person well or get him healed. In doing so, you and the doctor would then find yourselves fighting against God's will for that person. If you really believe that God's purpose was to put sickness upon the person, don't you go and try to get him made well. You should be cooperating with God, not working contrary to Him. Of course, when put it this way, most people realize how ridiculous this thinking actually is.

A couple of months ago, I wrote a letter to a man who had thought that God had placed a specific disease upon a particular woman to bear as a calling upon her life. My purpose was to explain to this man the concept of covenant; that if an exchange had truly taken place in the New Covenant, then the only way that we can interpret lingering sickness is that of the destructive work of the devil, which Yeshua came to destroy. Our posture then must be to come into agreement with Yeshua in this and fight the disease, not to come into agreement with or resignation to the illness. I think it may be useful in this discussion to quote below certain parts of this letter.

"Dear Bob (not his real name),

As I understand it, you conveyed to the woman that she was called by God to carry sickness in her body, and that in doing so she was perhaps entering into the fellowship of Christ's sufferings (Philippians 3:10). If this accurately describes what was conveyed, then it would indeed be very contrary to the teaching in the Bible for at least the following reasons.

1. In the New Covenant, into which we have been grafted, Jesus' blood was shed to pay for all iniquity, sin, sickness, and disease. This is taught in Isaiah 53:4-6. If Jesus paid for all sin and sickness, then to say that it is God's will to leave someone in sickness nullifies the New Covenant and declares that Jesus' blood was not sufficient to pay for sickness. Because God placed all of our disease and iniquity on Jesus, it would be illegal and a violation and nullification of the New Covenant for God to place or retain either iniquity or sickness upon a believer. In Matthew chapter 8 Jesus explains the meaning of Isaiah 53:4.

    Now when Jesus had come into Peter's house, He saw his wife's mother lying sick with a fever. So He touched her hand, and the fever left her. And she arose and served them. When evening had come, they brought to Him many who were demon-possessed. And He cast out the spirits with a word, and healed all who were sick, that it might be fulfilled which was spoken by Isaiah the prophet, saying: He Himself took our infirmities and bore our sicknesses. (Matthew 8:14-17)

Matthew 8:16 records that Jesus healed ALL who were sick. Not one time did Jesus ever leave someone in their sickness and tell them that it was God's will that they were to continue to bear their sickness. I would no more believe that God would place or retain sickness on a believer than I would believe that He would flood the earth again. I know this flood will not ever happen again from God because God made a covenant promise to Noah and declared that He would never again flood the earth. If someone told me that they heard God speak to them to tell someone that God was going to flood the whole earth, I would categorically reject that as not being from God, since it violates His word in the covenant He made with Noah. I would think exactly the same if someone told me that they thought that God told them that He had called them to carry sickness in their physical body. This would violate the New Covenant, of which we are partakers by the blood of Jesus.

2. *Bless the LORD, O my soul; and all that is within me, bless His holy name! Bless the LORD, O my soul, and forget not all His benefits: <u>Who forgives all your iniquities, Who heals all your diseases.</u>* (Psalm 103:1-3)

   Sickness and iniquity are spoken of together and were both 100% paid for by the blood of Jesus. Whatever you say about sickness, you would also have to say about iniquity. Psalm 103:3 says that He forgives ALL your iniquity and heals ALL your diseases. If one doubts that the blood of Jesus is sufficient to heal all one's diseases, one would also have to question if the blood of Jesus is sufficient to forgive all one's iniquities. Whatever is said of disease must be equally said of iniquity and sin. They are both in the same verse.

3. *God, who at various times and in various ways spoke in time past to the fathers by the prophets,*

has in these last days spoken to us by His Son, whom He has appointed heir of all things, through whom also He made the worlds; who being the brightness of His glory and the express image of His person, and upholding all things by the word of His power, when He had by Himself purged our sins, sat down at the right hand of the Majesty on high. (Hebrews 1:1-3)

We are told in this passage that God has spoken through the ages in many ways, but that in these last days, He has spoken to us by His Son, who is 'the express image of His person.' In other words, Jesus is the exact and perfect representation of the Father God. Thus, if it were God's will and purpose to place sickness upon people and ask them to carry it, we would find Jesus, when He walked on earth, doing exactly that in His representation of the Father. However, we cannot find one recorded incident in the Bible in which Jesus put sickness on anyone or retained him/her in it and told him/her that the sickness was of God. Actually, we find just the opposite (Matthew 4:23-24 and numerous other passages). If God now retains people in sickness and this is His will, then Jesus was not the express image of the Father's person, and He failed to show us a perfect representation of God. However, I am certain that Jesus was indeed the express image of the Father's person and that we are indeed to emulate His model of dealing with sickness...."

It is interesting to look at Yeshua's own understanding of His ambassadorship when He walked in physical form on earth. His "prayers" were quite different than many of ours today. The prayers of Yeshua for people were usually very short. They were actually not directed to God at all. They were frequently one word or short phrases that were the commands of an ambassador. Yeshua prayed things like,

"Peace be still;" "Go wash in the pool of Siloam;" "Stretch out your hand;" "Take up your bed and go home." Or how about this one? "Lazarus, come forth!" (Mark 4:39; John 9:7; Matthew 12:13; Mark 2:11; John 11:43) These were not the prayers of a private citizen begging the King for mercy or for help. These were the proclamations issued by an ambassador commanding people and circumstances to line up with the promises and policies made available by covenant.

It is incredible to think of what a difference this might make in our own lives if we were to really grasp the authority granted to us as ambassadors of the Kingdom of God, rather than being tourists. Apostle Peter apparently caught this revelation from watching Yeshua because he "prayed" for sick people in the same manner. After the resurrection of Messiah, Peter and John encountered a lame man at the temple entrance.

Then Peter said, "Silver and gold I do not have, but what I do have I give you: In the name of Jesus Christ of Nazareth, rise up and walk." And he took him by the right hand and lifted him up, and immediately his feet and ankle bones received strength. So he, leaping up, stood and walked and entered the temple with them— walking, leaping, and praising God. (Acts 3:6-8)

Many people who do not perceive themselves as ambassadors of the Kingdom, but rather as private citizens, perceive prayer then as begging God to do something that they want to have done. I am not saying that we are never to do this, as there certainly are times when it is entirely appropriate to come before the King with requests. However, there is another entire aspect of prayer into which many people have never entered due to their lack of understanding of their role as an ambassador. This entails intimate communication with our government (the King) and then using the delegated authority we have been given to release God's wisdom and power on the earth to accomplish His purpose. Then this aspect of prayer is not begging God as a private citizen, but rather speaking forth Kingdom proclamations for the purpose of using our authority to release God's power and wisdom to enforce Kingdom policy on earth. We will entertain a much more detailed discussion of the practicality of how to enter into this type of prayer in the next chapter of this book.

In Jesus' Name

Many times in the New Covenant writings of the Bible we see the phrase, "In Christ" or "In Him," or "In Jesus' name." What do these phrases mean? These actually are covenant terms that really have no meaning outside of the context of covenant. "In Christ" or "In Him" obviously does not mean that we are physically inside of Messiah. This phrase is a covenant phrase meaning we are His covenant representatives. It would be similar to saying He has granted us power of attorney to use His name as His representatives.

> He has granted us power of attorney to use His name as His representatives.

However, not understanding the concept of covenant or ambassadorship, we simply use this term as if it were just a tag on the end of a prayer. We frequently hear people pray and then conclude their prayer by saying, "In the name of Jesus." This really means to them, "And that's about all I have to say," or "I'm done praying now."

However, what this phrase actually means is, "Father, I am not coming before You today as Craig Hill, but rather the things that I have just said, I say as if I were Yeshua (Jesus). I am coming before You as His representative, not as a private citizen."

Most people can understand the concept of a power of attorney. This legal document gives one person the authority to act in behalf of another. Suppose you had a legitimate, signed, power of attorney document from Bill Gates, the founder of Microsoft, and a very wealthy man. With this document, you could go to Bill Gates' bank and request to withdraw ten million dollars from one of Mr. Gates' accounts. The bank teller might ask you, "Who are you to make such a request?" You would then answer, "Actually, it doesn't matter who I am. My name is inconsequential, because I am not coming to you today with this request in my name. I am coming to you today in the name of Bill Gates. And here is a signed document granting me the authority (power of attorney) to act on his behalf. My name doesn't matter, but his name does."

After examining the document and determining that it is indeed legitimate, the teller would then issue you the money. Now, many people would like to have such a document authorizing them to represent a very wealthy man. However, Yeshua has granted you the authority to use His name here on earth, which, of course, carries far more weight than that of a very wealthy man.

If you were to have such a document signed by Bill Gates, you would also need to realize you are obligated as a representative to carry out the wishes and policies of Bill Gates. If you simply used his authority and his money to do whatever you pleased without checking with Bill, you would probably not continue to be his representative for very long.

Thus, when we say, "in the name of Yeshua (Jesus)," we had better make sure that what we are saying and doing is actually authorized by Yeshua. If we truly understood this, we would not use this phrase so lightly at the end of our prayers.

I would thus encourage you to do a study in your Bible of the phrases "in Christ" and "in Him." This study would help you to grasp the actual privileges and responsibilities of your ambassadorship. As we grasp the incredible trust God has placed in us to be His ambassadors on earth, we then begin to take much more seriously our responsibility to remain in constant communication with Him. We would want to make sure that we are carrying out the duties assigned to us within our delegated sphere of influence.

With this understanding, we can now see how important it is to have a daily time of communication with our King through prayer and reading His Word. Can you imagine the problems we cause ourselves by forgetting or not being willing to check in with headquarters regularly, thereby missing out on a critical communiqué necessary to our lives or responsibilities? Even worse than this is not understanding the authority conveyed to us as God's ambassadors, and consequently responding to crisis or pressure as King Saul did, crying out, "What am I going to do?" instead of, "What has God said?"

Communiqués From Headquarters Are Essential

Many years ago, I was listening to a testimony given by a young woman on a television interview show. What she shared with the television audience was so impacting to me that I have never forgotten it. Her story was one of the most potent examples I have ever heard of the critical nature of understanding our role as ambassadors and keeping in regular communication with headquarters. I will recount below my recollection of this testimony as I heard it years ago.

The young woman was single and lived alone in an apartment in a major city in the United States. Being a New Covenant disciple of Yeshua, she had a habit of regularly reading her Bible and talking with the LORD every morning before work. She shared that one morning her daily reading included a passage from Isaiah 54. As she got to verses 14 and 15, the Holy Spirit strongly impressed her that she needed to memorize these verses and meditate upon them. She asked, "Why?" but didn't seem to get a clear answer. However, since it was such a strong impression of the Holy Spirit, she did so. The passage she was directed to memorize is as follows:

In righteousness you will be established; You will be far from oppression, for you will not fear; And from terror, for it will not come near you. If anyone fiercely assails you it will not be from Me. Whoever assails you will fall because of you. (Isaiah 54:14-15 NASB)

Several days later, in the early evening shortly after she came home from work, there was knock at the apartment door. As she opened the door, a man forced his way in, closed the door behind him, grabbed the young woman and put a knife to her throat. He then announced that he was going to rape her and that she had better cooperate. Faced with this sudden crisis, the young woman's mind began to race as to how to respond to this would-be rapist or maybe murderer.

Her first thought was of a news program she had watched not long ago detailing police statistics regarding murders, burglaries and rapes. The police had suggested that if one were ever confronted by an armed assailant, it would be wise to cooperate with him. Statistics had proven that such criminals were prone to kill their victims if resisted or provoked. Immediately following this thought came the scripture from Isaiah that she had recently memorized, and upon which she had been meditating. *"If anyone fiercely assails you it will not be from Me. Whoever assails you will fall because of you."* Now, she had a choice to make. How should she respond? She was just beginning to understand the release of God's power and wisdom through the exercise of her authority as His ambassador. However, she was also remembering the police statistics. It seemed that the stakes were very high, and a mistake in the wrong direction could cost her life.

A tourist mentality would be wondering, "Why did God 'allow' this to happen to me?" But this young woman had been meditating on the scripture passage that the Holy Spirit had quickened to her, and she immediately recognized that God had not allowed anything. This man was sent and motivated by the devil and the kingdom of darkness to destroy her. How did she know for sure? Very simply. God had just given her a "rhema" word for her life from the Bible whereby He had said, *"If anyone fiercely assails you it will not be from Me. Whoever assails you will fall because of you."* And now, here was someone fiercely assailing her. So she immediately knew that this was not from God. She further knew from this word that she was not to accept this, but rather to resist it. God had given her a rhema word that she would not fall, but rather that the man would fall because of her. It takes a long time to relate this story, but in the circumstance this entire thought sequence only took a second to process.

In the first moment, the young woman shared that she had felt a knot of fear and terror hit her stomach with the surprise of the attack. However, just as quickly, rising up out of her spirit came the first part of the word that God had given her, *"In righteousness you will be established; You will be far from oppression, for you will not fear; And from terror, for it will not come near you."* As this word came into her mind and she embraced it, she felt the fear and terror simply melt away.

With this rhema word from God so strongly implanted in her spirit, she now easily decided, as David probably did the first time when confronted with a lion in the shepherd's field, to run toward the lion, rather than away from it. Consequently, the young woman turned her head toward the man as he had announced, "I'm going to rape you," and said, "No, you're not! I'm a blood covenant partner with the Lord Jesus Christ. That means that Jesus and I are one. I am in Him and He is in me. That means that whatever you do to me, you do to Him. What have you come here today to do? Rape Jesus Christ?"

The man was so shocked that he didn't know how to respond. She reported that he looked at her as if he were an actor in a play and wanted to say to her, "No, no, no, no! You are not playing your part correctly. You can't say that. You see, I am the rapist and you are the victim. I push into your apartment. You scream. I put the knife to your throat and you cooperate with me as I rape you. You scream. You cry. You are filled with fear and terror. No, no, no! You are doing this all wrong. You are not supposed to say that! Now you have messed up the whole scene." In actuality, all he could say was, "What?"

She then continued, "You see, I am the apple of God's eye. Apple is a Hebrew idiom for the word pupil. Right now, you have your finger in the pupil of God's eye. Do you want to continue to mess with God Almighty?"

The man then regained a little of his composure and stated, "If you don't cooperate with me, I'm going to kill you."

The young woman simply continued, "I don't know if you can kill me or not. However, it doesn't matter to me because my life doesn't belong to me. My life is in the hands of God my Father. If today is my day to die, I am fine with that. No problem."

The man tried everything he knew to do to frighten her and get her to embrace fear and terror. However, it was too late, as the rhema word from God was already much too strong within her. She wouldn't move into tourist mode as a private citizen to deal with him on her own in fear. She just continued to stand her ground as an ambassador. By this time, the man himself was trembling and said, "You don't understand. I'm serious."

She said, "So am I. I am trying to spare you from cursing your life and making yourself God's enemy. You need to understand that I am an ambassador of the Most High God. Again, what you do to me, you do to Him. You will account to God for the way in which you treat me, His ambassador. If you harm me, let me assure you that you will curse your own life with God, and make yourself His enemy."

"Furthermore," she continued, "you have no authority here. This is not your apartment. God gave it to me to manage for Him. Therefore, you are currently trespassing on

God's property. I am not personally telling you, but as an ambassador, I command you in the Name of the Lord Jesus Christ to vacate the premises."

Finally the man released her, ran out the door, and fled from her apartment, leaving her unharmed. Shortly after this, the rapist was apparently caught by police, tried and imprisoned. As with David and the lion, I believe there was an explosion in her spirit as the man ran out the door. "Yes! The Word of God is true. I really am His ambassador and the word of my King really does have authority on earth."

I am convinced that in order for the demonic force working through the rapist to function, it must stimulate fear in the victim. If it cannot use the man to stimulate fear, it is not able to function, and the man cannot complete his demonic assignment. Fear and terror create the operative environment that must be present in order for such a spirit to function. When this woman refused to enter that environment of terror and continued to exercise her authority as an ambassador, it made it almost impossible for the man to complete his mission of terrorizing and raping her.

Probably at this point you can see how important is was for this young woman not to miss her appointed time of reading the word of God and praying each day. Suppose she didn't have time to read her Bible the day that Isaiah 54 was in her reading. Perhaps God could have found another way to get that rhema word to her, so she would have the bicycle knowledge she would need regarding someone fiercely assailing her. However, it was most easy to do through her regular daily appointment to check in as an ambassador with her government headquarters.

Another very important point to realize is how important it was for the young woman to be sensitive and obedient to the Holy Spirit. In the situation with the rapist, she could not afford to be a stranger to the covenant promise that God made real to her personally from Isaiah 54:14-15. She could not afford to be like King Saul, having read the word but not meditating upon it. Remember, a covenant will do you no good unless all three things are true. In this young woman's case, they were.

1) She had entered into the New Covenant.

2) She had meditated upon the specific promise of the covenant that would be necessary to her so that she knew it (bicycle knowledge); and

3) She had enough confidence from meditating on the covenant promise that when crisis came to her life, she was willing to enforce the word of God as an ambassador against an enemy.

Interpreting Life's Experiences

Now imagine the interpretation of such an experience in the life of another young woman who also may have had the same would-be rapist break into her apartment. Suppose that she, like this first one, was also a New Covenant disciple. Suppose, however, that for whatever reason, this second young woman was still a stranger to the covenant promise and was walking through life as a tourist, rather than an ambassador. When the rapist pushed into her apartment and put the knife to her throat, suppose that she became filled with fear and began to scream and cry out to Jesus to help her. With this woman now behaving as the rapist wanted her to, he proceeds to rape her and leaves her emotionally devastated in a heap on the floor of her apartment.

Now, how would we interpret the two life experiences of these two women with the same rapist? What was the difference between the two women? They both were in covenant with the same God. He had given them both the same Bible and the same covenant promises. They had both read Isaiah 54. The same blood of Messiah Yeshua had been shed for each of them. The pertinent heart questions are: Does God love them both the same, or is God indeed a respecter of persons?

Let's now return to the model of the four different presuppositions regarding God's responsibility and justice that we looked at in chapter four. Remember that presupposition number one sees life from the perspective that God is in control and therefore is responsible for the event and that the event is just. He "allowed" the second woman to be raped, while He protected the first woman. From this perspective, how do we not see God as a respecter of persons who apparently loved or favored the first woman more than the second?

If the second woman herself sees life from this first presupposition and believes that God is in control, she may have a very difficult time with not letting her heart get angry and bitter toward God. There is always a lingering question in her heart, "God, why did you let this happen to me?" If she then hears the testimony of the first woman, she may truly feel that God really does have favorites, and she is not one of them. The question in her heart would be, "Why was the first woman not raped by the criminal and I was? God you protected her and you let it happen to me. Where were you?"

After this experience, for this second woman it will be difficult for her not to slip into presupposition number two, that sees life from the perspective that God is in control and is responsible for the event, and that the event was not just. The conclusion of this second position then, is that God is not just. He is in control, and like a cruel puppet master, He unfairly protects some while He allows others to be devastated. This then is a set-up for a huge well of hidden disappointment, resentment and anger toward God in her heart

It would be quite different, however, if we looked at this event from the perspective of presupposition number four. This position sees life from that perspective, that God is not responsible for the event. This man is motivated by and was serving the kingdom of darkness. He was not God's puppet or agent. God is not "allowing" this, but rather, Yeshua came to destroy such works, not to authorize them (1 John 3:8). Secondly, this attack is not just, but rather is evil and completely unjust. From this perspective, we would not see God as being responsible for the rapist pushing his way into either woman's apartment. We would rather see this as one of the works of the devil that Yeshua came to destroy (1 John 3:8). We would see God as no respecter of persons. He loves both women exactly the same and has made the opportunity available to both women to get a revelation of the authority that He has made available to them as His ambassadors. However, the first woman has bicycle knowledge of the covenant promise that she will need to deal with her assailant, while the second woman has not. Then from this perspective, it really becomes true in practical reality that people perish, or are destroyed for lack of knowledge (Hosea 4:6).

Because I do see life from this fourth presupposition, when I realized the reality of Hosea 4:6, I initially became very fearful. I thought to myself, "Oh, my goodness! There are all kinds of promises in the Bible that I might have read, but I know I don't yet have true inner bicycle knowledge of these."

You may be thinking, "I don't know what I would have done if a rapist were to break into my home when I was there all alone. I probably would have responded like the second woman." Fear then sets in, because you suddenly realize that you are a stranger to the promises of God's covenant. You recognize that in many areas of God's promises, you have no true bicycle knowledge, which is strong enough inside to empower you to have the confidence to confront an enemy and enforce the policy of your King. As I meditated upon this thought, I heard the Holy Spirit tell me, "Son, you don't need to have bicycle knowledge of every promise of the covenant right now. You just need to have knowledge of the one that I direct you to today or this week.""

The key point was not that I needed to have to have a true inner image of every promise of the covenant, but rather that I needed to pursue an intimate relationship daily and moment by moment with the LORD. Through regular appointments and intimate fellowship, He could then direct me to the things I would need to know for that day, week or month. The first woman, who actually had the experience with the would-be rapist, had been given by the Holy Spirit several days prior exactly the scripture verse that contained the covenant promise that she needed for that circumstance. She probably didn't have a rhema revelational word for the healing of cancer. That was not what she needed that week. Once I understood this, it set my heart at peace to realize that I don't need to know every promise of covenant. I just need to walk as an ambassador and not a tourist. If I maintain regular intimacy with Him and not miss the regular appointments I have made with Him, the LORD can then impart to me the instructions I will need to carry out my duties as His ambassador that day.

Your Son Has the Most Serious Head Injury I've Ever Seen

In conclusion of this discussion, I'd like to share a personal experience that occurred in our family several years ago and reinforced these truths to me. At the time of this event, I was pastoring a church and had just taught a sermon series on the authority of the blood covenant. Over the spring school holidays, our family had gone to Steamboat Springs, Colorado on a ski/snowboard vacation. The second day of our holiday, our two sons, Josh and Jonathan, had gone off to snowboard on their own, as Jan and I were usually too slow for them.

On the third or fourth run of the day, Jan and I came up to the top of the chairlift, where we noticed my name written on a notice board with a message directing me to go to the nearest ski patrol office. As Jan and I walked over to the ski patrol shack at the top of the mountain, we wondered what could have happened. Usually this is an indication that someone in your party has broken a leg or been injured. As we walked, fear began to mount that perhaps Josh or Jonathan could have been hurt.

As we arrived at the ski patrol shack, I knocked on the door. One of the ski patrolwomen opened the door, and I told her that the message board had directed me to the ski patrol. She asked my name, and as soon as I told her, she looked very concerned, turned around to another patrolman behind her and said, "You had better tell them." I thought, "Oh my! What do they have to tell us?" This is not the news that any parent wants to receive on a ski holiday. The man

163

came to the door and proceeded to tell us that Josh, who was 15 years old at the time, had had a snowboarding accident. He proceeded to tell us that about forty-five minutes ago, Josh had gone off a jump on his snowboard, lost control in the air, and had landed on his head on some very hard ice.

Apparently the sun had been out in the afternoon the day before, and the snow below the jump had melted and turned to slush. Then in the cold temperature overnight, the slush had frozen into very solid, hard ice. The patrolman continued by telling us that he had personally been on the scene shortly after it happened, and that he had observed Josh, unconscious, with his arms and legs flailing spastically about, literally like a chicken with its head cut off. They had had to sedate Josh and get him down to the local hospital as quickly as possible. The patrolman told us that Josh was now in town in the hospital, but that we had better get down there as soon as possible because he was certain that they would need to airlift him to Denver for neurosurgery on his brain. He said, "In all the years that I have been on the ski patrol here, your son has the most severe brain injury that I have ever seen."

When you receive news like this, as a parent your being is immediately flooded with emotion and adrenaline. Within a few seconds, I immediately remembered several parts of the teaching that I had just given at our church on the blood covenant. The thought never even entered Jan's or my mind, "Why would God allow this to happen to our son?" We knew that this had nothing to do with God, but rather was a work of the enemy. We immediately recognized that this was a strategy of Satan and the kingdom of darkness to harm Josh, attack us and stop what we as a family were doing in the Kingdom of God. I knew that it had been no accident that I had just taught the series on blood covenant and ambassadorship in our church. This teaching had contained the rhema word that we needed right at that moment to deal with this situation. One scripture verse that came to me very quickly on the mountain was James 4:7.

Therefore submit to God. Resist the devil and he will flee from you. (James 4:7)

The enemy had tried to take our son out, and I was now militantly angry. Jan and I stopped and briefly prayed before we started down the mountain. I did not ask God to heal my son. I realized that this work had already been accomplished two thousand years ago when Yeshua was raised from the dead. We didn't need to ask God to do that. We just needed to use our authority as His ambassadors to release God's power in Josh's life to destroy the

> I did not ask God to heal my son. I realized that this work had already been accomplished two thousand years ago when Yeshua was raised from the dead.

works of the enemy (1 John 3:8), and to manifest the healing Yeshua had already purchased for him by His blood.

So understanding James 4:7, we first submitted ourselves to God. We poured out a little of the emotion we were feeling to Yeshua. We then told the LORD that we understood we were His ambassadors and were prepared to do whatever was necessary for His Kingdom rule and reign to come into this situation, and for His will to be done *("Let Your Kingdom come and Your will be done, on earth as it is in heaven;* Matthew 6:10). We began to proclaim God's will for healing for Josh's brain and physical body to be manifested on earth, even as it was already completed in God's sight in heaven.

Having submitted to God, we then resisted the devil and his strategy in our son's life and commanded him to flee from Josh. I also let the enemy know that as a result of this attack, I would now double my effort in expanding the Kingdom of God and taking people out of his camp. Whenever I perceive a direct attack of the enemy against my family or me, I have always had a very militant attitude rise up from my spirit that says, "If you do that, I will double what I was doing to destroy your works in the earth, and to expand the Kingdom of God."

We then quickly skied down the mountain to the base and then, as rapidly as we could, drove to the hospital. When we arrived, they told us that a doctor was attending to Josh and he was having a CAT scan done to try to determine the extent of the damage to his brain. They took us into a private waiting room and told us that indeed they would have to airlift Josh to Denver to one of the larger hospitals for brain surgery. I could accompany him in the plane and Jan would return to our condominium, gather all our belongings and drive the car back to Denver. The nurse then asked us if we would like to see a "clergyman." Jan told her, "No, I think we'll be OK. My husband is a pastor." We simply requested that we would like to pray for Josh before he was taken to the airplane for transport to the hospital in Denver. Realizing the serious nature of the circumstance, we called our Family Foundations (FFI) office and asked our staff to mobilize the FFI intercessors around to world to pray for Josh as well. We were later shocked at how many of our FFI ministry family around the world had prayed for Josh with specific direction they had received from the LORD.

Both Jan and I were glad that they didn't send a chaplain in to "comfort" us. We realized that we were in the midst of a battle, and we needed to be ready to use the authority that

God had given us as His ambassadors to release His power on Josh's behalf to destroy the works of the enemy. We certainly didn't need someone who had no understanding of ambassadorship, Kingdom authority, or of the battle at hand, telling us that what had happened to Josh was God's will. We certainly did not need someone telling us things such as "God is in control" or "We don't know why God allows such things, but we just have to accept that His ways are higher than our ways. We just have to submit to whatever He wants for your son." That would be like having a "comforter" or military advisor come and tell you falsely that your commanding General had already surrendered and given you into the hands of your enemy, just as you are getting ready to confront the enemy in battle.

After a short while, the doctor came into our room and showed us a couple of CAT scan pictures. He told us that he saw two areas of concern in Josh's brain that would probably need neurosurgery when he got to the hospital in Denver. He again emphasized that the head injury was very serious, and that Josh needed to be airlifted to Denver as quickly as possible. Josh had been sedated and his respiration and heart had been taken over by machines to ensure that he would continue to breathe and have blood circulation. We then asked if we could see Josh and pray over him. The doctor told us that we could do so in just a couple of minutes.

After a few minutes, they wheeled Josh's bed into our room and told us that we could pray for him. Josh's face was badly scraped up from the ice. There were tubes protruding from everywhere, and he was hooked up to all kinds of machines. We, however, did not look on his outward appearance, but rather just focused on what we were called to do as God's Kingdom ambassadors. So we stood over him, laid our hands on his head and proclaimed God's covenant

167

word that Yeshua had died to heal the damage to his brain from the accident. We commanded health to come to every cell of Josh's brain and released the blood of Yeshua to touch the damaged areas, reduce swelling, and heal. We then revoked any authority that the devil or any demonic spirit might have thought they had over Josh and opened the door for God's healing power to be released in Josh's physical body. After we had prayed, it was then time to take Josh by ambulance to the airport to be airlifted to Denver.

I rode with Josh in the ambulance and climbed onboard the Cessna 421 twin-engine airplane to ride to Denver. The flight nurse then boarded the airplane, and we took off. The flight was less than an hour, but a couple times along the way the nurse seemed to be concerned about Josh's vital signs. He said a couple of times, "Come on buddy, you can make it." Each time I continued to pray and release God's power in Josh's life. Finally, we arrived at the airport in Denver, were loaded into another ambulance and whisked away to Swedish Medical Center.

When we arrived at the hospital in Denver, they immediately took Josh to ICU and began to conduct more scans, tests and do an overall examination. After a couple of hours had gone by, the trauma doctor was the first to come give me an updated report. He told me that after a thorough examination they had determined that in addition to the closed head injury, Josh had a ruptured spleen and a broken left elbow. He told us that they hoped to be able to save the spleen, but that they had to be very careful to monitor his blood count so that he would not bleed to death internally. I thanked the doctor for the report and now had additional information by which to pray.

Soon after this, the neurosurgeon came with her report. She said after more CAT scans and MRI scans, it seemed that the two areas of swelling and damage which had shown up on the CAT scans from Steamboat Springs were no longer evident and that no surgery would be required. She couldn't really explain why there was such a significant difference between the CAT scans from a few hours ago and the ones now, but she just said that it is very difficult to predict what will happen with closed head injuries. "Sometimes something in the brain sort of heals itself unexplainably," she said. She went on to say that Josh had received about the most severe concussion that one could experience, but that there was nothing that would require surgery, and we would simply have to wait to see what sort of permanent damage there might be.

Of course, I knew what had caused such a difference between to two CAT scans a few hours apart. It was the healing power of God released through the words of our authority spoken into Josh's life in the hospital in Steamboat Springs. Later that evening, Jan arrived at the hospital, having driven back with our car. One of us continued to stay with Josh at all times over the next week as he recovered in the hospital. Already, the next morning Josh was conscious, although he remained asleep most of the time as his body recovered from the severe trauma he had undergone. We continued to use the words of our mouths as ambassadors to release into Josh's life the healing that Yeshua had purchased by His blood. We also proclaimed healing to his spleen and elbow.

About a week later, Josh was released to go home from the hospital. The doctors were amazed at his rapid and remarkable recovery. They did not have to remove his spleen and his elbow healed very quickly. In the end, Josh experienced no permanent damage to his brain from the accident. There was, however, one interesting side affect.

Josh had always had a "lazy eye" that would turn inward and cross when he would get tired. The eye doctor had instructed us to place a patch over the other eye for much of his waking hours for a couple years when he was seven or eight years old. Even after patching the other eye, the "lazy eye" had never completely been corrected. However, after this snowboard accident, we never observed in Josh that "lazy eye" again. It was completely healed.

I am totally convinced that the outcome of this accident in Josh's life may have been very different had Jan and I not understood the battle at hand, and had we not been prepared to take our role as ambassadors. The LORD had prepared us by the sermon series I had just taught on the power and authority of blood covenant. We were also prepared by our understanding the difference between the prayer of an ambassador and that of a tourist. In the next chapter, let's look at how the concept of being an ambassador may affect the way in which we pray.

Reflection

1. Most people have spent their lives living as tourists and have never received their charge as Kingdom ambassadors.

2. Covenant has created a divine exchange: Messiah's life for ours.

3. God will never act contrary to His covenant word.

4. Yeshua has granted us power of attorney to use His name on earth.

5. As ambassadors, it is critical for us to remain in regular communication with headquarters, so as not to miss an important communiqué.

6. In what areas of your life have you behaved more like a tourist than an ambassador?

Resources

🎧 Ambassador or Tourist? (Single CD Teaching)

chapter 8
IF GOD IS IN CONTROL, THEN WHY PRAY?

n this chapter we want to consider how the idea that "God is in control" potentially impacts motivation for and understanding of prayer. For the first few years in my covenant relationship with Yeshua, I had only understood prayer as presenting my requests to God. At that time, I viewed life much more from the perspective of presupposition number one that God was in control. Consequently, I would come to God with a list of things that I desired for Him to act on. However, after some time, I began to think about my relationship with God in prayer. I really wanted to know why I was praying and what prayer actually accomplished, besides making me feel like I had completed a religious duty or discipline.

I began to seek to understand what to me was the mystery of prayer. I understood praise and worship of God. I understood relational conversation with God, letting Him know how I felt and listening to His heart. However, what I didn't understand was prayer to make requests of God for myself or for others. I had reasoned that since God was in control, He already knew everything that I was requesting from Him before I asked. So what was I doing? Was I trying to convince God to do something that He really didn't want to do? Was I advising God of some information of which He was unaware? Was God qualifying me before He would move, such that if I begged long enough and was persistent enough, He would finally get up off His couch and do something? Was I trying to convince God that I was really, really serious, and if I was serious enough, God would do what I was asking? Or, was prayer actually doing nothing in regards to God, but was really just for my benefit to make me feel like I was connected to Him and God was listening to me?

In my quest to understand prayer, I asked many people why we should pray and what we were doing. Most shared with me clichés such as "prayer changes things," "prayer is powerful," and "prayer moves the hand of God." However, when I would ask people <u>why</u> these things were true, it seemed that I didn't receive very satisfactory answers. No one seemed to really know. Or if they did, they couldn't explain it to me. They all thought prayer was very important, but couldn't tell me why.

I had been taught and believed that God already knew everything, and that He was the One with the power to change things. What made no sense to me was that if He already knows my needs and the needs of others around me, then why am I telling Him about our needs? Secondly, I don't have any power to change anything because God is the One with all the power. Thirdly, I can't see the big picture, and God has all the wisdom regarding timing and how this request might impact the entire universe and everyone in it. "If God knows everything, has all the power, has all the wisdom, and He is in control, surely He will just do whatever He sees fit that needs to be done in His timing. Right?" I reasoned.

My job as His servant, I thought, was to be a good trooper, not complain about evil and injustice that He allows to afflict my life and the lives of those around me, and to accept the manner and timing in which He chooses to orchestrate my life. This conclusion for me was very demotivating for prayer. I didn't feel like I was accomplishing anything by talking to God about people, circumstances, or needs about which He already knew and already had in control. So I didn't pray much after embracing this conclusion. I knew I should, but I didn't know why.

Finally, in 1975 I began to find a little breakthrough in my experience of prayer. I found myself at a short-term summer mission training camp in Holland with Youth With a Mission (YWAM). One of the things we were taught that summer was a concept of prayer that was completely new to me. We were taught first of all that we could actually expect to hear God speak His thoughts right into our minds. With this understanding, we were then taught to ask God what was on His heart for us to pray, and then to speak forth in prayer those things that He brought to our minds.

I was thrilled with this concept of prayer because it was much more interactive than just presenting our requests to God. This style of prayer also seemed much more participatory in that we were first listening to God's voice, and then partnering with Him to pray out those things that He brought to our minds. So we were not just praying the things that we wanted God to do. We were actually finding out what was important to Him and praying out these things. In addition, many times we were receiving natural confirmation that the things we had prayed had actually come to pass. I began to feel that in praying this way, we

175

were actually making a difference. Our prayers were actually accomplishing something in partnership with God. However, I still didn't understand why this style of prayer was effective and what we were doing.

This type of prayer really seemed circular to me. My reasoning was as follows. God knows what needs to be done. He then tells us what is on His heart that needs to be prayed. We then tell God the things that He told us. Since we have no power, and He has all the power, the Holy Spirit then goes forth and uses His power to accomplish the things that we just prayed. The part that made no sense to me was **why doesn't God just cut out the middleman?** Since He knows what needs to be done, and He has the power and wisdom to do it, why does He need to tell us, so we can tell Him, so He can do it? Why doesn't He just go do what He knows needs to be done? I don't know if you have ever entertained thoughts like this, but this dilemma really perplexed me.

Another aspect of intercession also perplexed me. I heard teaching on intercessory prayer regarding the fact that it was very important to God to find intercessors who would stand in the gap and pray for others. The Bible teachers I was listening to quoted scriptures such as Isaiah 59:16, Isaiah 63:5, and Ezekiel 22:30. In these passages, prophets tell us that God was actually astonished and wondered at the fact that He sought for an intercessor, but could find none. It's interesting to ponder what would astonish God. Apparently the lack of intercessors is one thing that is amazing or astonishing to Him.

So I sought for a man among them who would make a wall, and stand in the gap before Me on behalf of the land, that I should not destroy it; but I found no one. (Ezekiel 22:30)

Now the LORD saw, and it was displeasing in His sight that there was no justice. And He saw that there was no man, And was astonished that there was no one to intercede. (Isaiah 59:15b-16a NASB)

I understood from these scriptures that it was very important to God to partner with men and women on earth as intercessors to accomplish His purposes. But I still didn't understand the reason. Furthermore, I had heard many dynamic testimonies regarding God waking up intercessors in the middle of the night to pray for people in other parts of the world. The things that the intercessor had prayed were later confirmed as having had a real impact by the people for whom the prayer had gone forth. I remember one situation in which a missionary in Nepal was riding on an airplane in a very dangerous situation. Intercessors were awakened in the middle of the night and led to pray for the physical safety of the missionary half a world away. Later, the missionary confirmed that he was indeed riding on an airplane and was in a very perilous situation with bad weather and equipment failure in Nepal at exactly the time and day that the intercessors had been awakened. The missionary reported God's supernatural intervention in the circumstance which resulted in the airplane not crashing and his life being spared.

As I heard many such testimonies, I was thrilled by the fact that intercessors seemed to be actually making a difference through their prayers, but I still couldn't understand what the intercessors were doing or why they were necessary. My reasoning again was that God had all knowledge, power, and wisdom. Surely He knew that the plane on which the missionary was riding was in trouble. It was also His supernatural intervention that spared the missionary's life. So why did God need to wake people up in Colorado in the middle of the night to intercede for the missionary in Nepal? Since God was in control, He knew of the problem, and had the wisdom and power to solve the problem, so why didn't God just move supernaturally to solve the problem? This was my question.

So What Really Is Answered Prayer?

If you have read the last several chapters of this book, you probably already know the answer to the theological dilemma I was facing. This dilemma, of course, was solved for me when I realized that God is not in control, but that He is sovereign. I further began to see life much more from the perspective of presupposition number four rather than number one. This position says that God is not responsible for evil and injustice on the earth because He has delegated authority to man. Understanding intercession from the perspective of an ambassador rather than a tourist changes the total understanding of what we are doing in intercessory prayer. Many of the questions I was asking regarding prayer were answered by seeing life from this perspective.

> God lacks authority. This is because He has delegated authority to man by covenant.

Remember from chapter three the understanding that God has knowledge, wisdom, power, and love. What does He lack? God lacks authority. This is because He has delegated authority to man by covenant. This delegation then makes us His ambassadors on the earth. As such, we are called by God to speak His word, which releases authority for Him to act supernaturally in power and wisdom. So why does God need intercessors? Because He lacks the authority delegated to man to justly release His power on earth. For this reason, God wakes people up in the middle of the night to pray for someone in another part of the world. He knows what needs to happen, and the Holy Spirit and sometimes angels have been dispatched with power to accomplish the task, but no power can be released until a redeemed human on earth opens the door of authority to release the power.

With this understanding from presupposition number four, I could then understand the seemingly circular prayer. We were to seek God to access His knowledge and wisdom. We could then combine that with our delegated authority by using the words of our mouths to release His power to accomplish the task. So again, we find that God's purpose is to draw us into relationship and partnership with Him.

If this is really true, and it is, can you imagine the bottleneck that our lack of knowledge (Hosea 4:6) must create in Heaven? God sees the strategies of the enemy on the earth and is seeking to destroy the works of the devil (1 John 3:8). But if many members of the body of Messiah have never learned to ask God what is on His heart and then pray in partnership with Him to release His power through their authority, then many things in the heart of God go undone on the earth. So people perish, the enemy wins battles, evil and injustice prevail in situations, and God is blamed by disciples and unbelievers alike for the works of the devil because:

- Many believe that "God is in control."

- Many have never understood or received their commission as ambassadors.

- Many are consequently wandering through life as tourists.

- Many are yet strangers to the covenants of promise.

- Many have not yet understood their Covenant relationship with God.

- Many have no idea that God has delegated authority to us and, therefore, that He needs to access our authority on earth to act.

- Many are begging God to act, rather than exercising their authority to declare and release Kingdom policy on earth.

King Saul was waiting for God to do something, or at least for a huge, strong warrior to show up. David released God's authority with his words and a simple action, and God defeated the Philistine enemies of Israel. Dr. Benson Idahosa did not wait for God to do something about the witchcraft conference in his city. He listened to the voice of the Father, and then as an ambassador simply proclaimed the policy of Heaven and relied upon God to back up the word given to His ambassador. The young woman who was assaulted by the would-be rapist in her apartment was not begging God to do something. She simply proclaimed the Covenant word God had given her and watched the confidence and power drain out of the assailant like air out of a balloon. In the face of her covenant authority, he cowered and ran from her place of appointed jurisdiction.

This understanding that covenant disciples are ambassadors actually reverses the traditional language and thinking about this type of prayer. We oftentimes hear people talk about "answered" prayer. From the standpoint of ambassadors, we are actually the ones doing the answering. God wants to speak to us and has many things that He would like us to proclaim and release on earth. Thus, He is waiting for us to listen and answer Him. I believe that the greatest problem in accomplishing God's Kingdom purpose on the earth is not getting God to answer us, but rather getting us to listen to and answer Him. So true answered prayer is when we finally pick up the line to heaven and answer God's request of us as His ambassadors.

What do you think might happen if everyone who reads this book were simply to dedicate one hour per week to ask God what is on His heart and pray it forth as an ambassador? What if you simply took one hour per week and said to God, "Father, if You were looking for someone from redeemed humanity, in covenant with You, willing to make proclamations

> So true answered prayer is when we finally pick up the line to heaven and answer God's request of us as His ambassadors.

in prayer as your ambassador today, look no further. I am available to You for the next hour. I am ready to listen to Your voice. Anything You would like me, (or if gathered in a group, us) to pray, here I am (we are)." Then wait, listen, and speak forth what He shows you. I believe that if we did this, we would see an explosion of the Kingdom of God.

How God Can Be Impartially Partial

In order for God to be truly just on the earth, what He does for one, He must be willing to do for all. However, many times when there is a tragedy involving many people such as an earthquake, hurricane, an act of terrorism, or a bridge collapse, we hear stories of supernatural intervention by God in the lives of various people. These people will then testify of the supernatural timing and intervention by God in their lives. However, there are also others involved in the tragedy who have no such testimony, and in fact perished instead. So what about these people? Did God love the first ones more, or is God a respecter of persons and spared some, while He let others perish? Is God unjust? You would be tempted to think so if it were your loved one who perished.

I believe that one of the answers to this is the fact that prayer opens the door for God to be impartially partial. As an ambassador, prayer opens the door of authority for God to be able to intervene supernaturally in the life of the person prayed for, whereas He has no such authority to do so in the life of another person for whom no ambassador opened the door of authority in prayer. Many times when we look a little deeper into the testimony of the one who was spared, we find people who were led at that exact time to pray for that person, even though they had no natural human knowledge as to why.

A few years ago, one of our FFI ministry teams in Manaus, Brazil, shared with us such a story. The team left Manaus on a riverboat going up the Amazon River to a smaller town for the purpose of conducting an Ancient Paths seminar. Shortly after midnight, in the wee hours of the morning, one of the team members was awakened and felt like the LORD told her to stay awake and be alert. Not long after that, the riverboat apparently collided with some sort of debris in the water and capsized. Most of the passengers on board were asleep.

The young woman who was awakened by the LORD was able to quickly exit her bed and get out of the boat. She found some debris in the water and grabbed onto it for flotation. She immediately began to pray for the other team members, as she knew that there was at least one other woman who did not know how to swim. Amazingly, within the next few minutes she spied that woman a short distance away. This other woman seemed to sort of float over to her and she then helped her grab hold of the same floating debris. These two women were then able to make their way to shore, which at that point in the huge river, was several miles.

A large number of the passengers lost their lives in that particular riverboat accident that night. However, all five of the FFI team members made it safely to shore, including the one woman who didn't even know how to swim. This second woman, when asked how she got out of the flooded, sinking boat, told us the following account.

She was fast asleep when the riverboat capsized. However, she woke up when the boat pitched upside down. She then reported that a man in a white robe reached down through the water and grabbed her by the hand and pulled her out through the corridor of the boat and into the open water. He then upheld her on the water until she saw her friend and was then deposited on the floating debris with her other team member.

When the team later reached a town with a telephone, they began to ring their friends and family to let them know that they were not harmed. Several of their friends and family members asked them at exactly what time the accident had occurred. These ones then reported that the LORD had woken them up in the middle of the night and told them to pray for the safety of their friend or relative and for the entire FFI team traveling that night on the riverboat. Some of the intercessors had been given more details by the LORD than others, but several reported being wakened to pray and had done so.

Why was an angel released to pull the one woman from the sinking boat to safety on the floating debris with her teammate? I believe that it was due to the intercession of her friends and relatives. They were woken by the LORD and called to intercede as ambassadors to release God's Kingdom purpose for her life and to destroy the work of the enemy, who was intent on killing her that night. Why were there no angels to help the more than one hundred people who drowned that night on the same boat? I don't know for sure, but perhaps one reason is that there were no ambassadors found to personally intercede for them. This may not be the entire explanation, but I am certain that intercession as ambassadors has a lot to do with this.

We see a scriptural example of angels being released to do battle with agents of the kingdom of darkness in the book of Daniel chapter ten. In this passage, an angel tells Daniel that he was released to come to earth through Daniel's intercessory prayer.

Then he said to me, "Do not fear, Daniel, for from the first day that you set your heart to understand, and to humble yourself before your God, your words were heard; and I have come because of your words. But the prince of the kingdom of Persia withstood me twenty-one days; and behold, Michael, one of the chief princes, came to help me, for I had been left alone there with the kings of Persia (Daniel 10:12-13).

We see here that intercessory prayer for others as directed by the LORD is critical as to the outcome of the events taking place in the lives of men and women on planet earth. I was shocked to find out that the LORD had led my wife Jan to pray for me when I was in a very dangerous situation six months before we even met. I believe that her prayer released authority for God to move supernaturally to save my life. I have included below a passage recounting this story from my book *Two Fleas and No Dog*[1].

Low Fuel

In the course of talking with each other, I was very surprised to find out that God had led Jan to pray for me in a very specific way six months before we had even met. Although she didn't know at the time that it was me she was praying for, God had led her in a very supernatural way to participate in saving my life. Let me share with you how that had happened.

In early 1975, I had just graduated from college and had a nine-month period of time before I would start a two-year graduate MBA program in Chicago. For the first few months of the year, I was employed as a copilot in a Learjet flying the US mail out of Grand Rapids, Michigan five nights a week. We would leave Grand Rapids around midnight and fly to Chicago, Bloomington, Illinois and on to St. Louis. Then we would fly back through Peoria, Illinois, Chicago again and then back across Lake Michigan to Grand Rapids. One night, on the last leg of the trip from Chicago back to Grand Rapids, the Chicago Air Traffic Control Center advised us that the weather in much of Michigan was deteriorating very rapidly with fog and low visibility. He suggested that we might want to return to Chicago.

---

[1] Hill, Craig. *Two Fleas and No Dog*. Littleton: Family Foundations International. 2007. pp. 86-91

The captain and I looked at each other, and he asked me, "Do you want to go back to Chicago?"

"No," I answered. "If we do, we'll probably get stuck in the pilots' lounge all day. I'm tired. I want to go home and go to bed. I bet we can beat the fog into Grand Rapids."

He concurred with me. We told the Air Traffic Control that we would continue to Grand Rapids.

I don't know why, but I have noticed that frequently they locate airports right in the crook of a river. This is the case in Grand Rapids, Michigan. So where does the fog form first? Right over the river, of course, which is right on the approach end of the precision instrument approach runway. As a result, we had discovered that when the visibility was low, many times we could get into the airport on the non-precision instrument approach from the non-river end of the runway more easily even though the visibility and altitude minimums were higher than they were from the other direction.

This particular night, we shot the first instrument approach with no success. When we arrived at the minimum altitude we saw no runway, no lights, no ground; nothing but fog. So we ascended and tried the precision approach from the other direction. On descent on the second approach, two little red lights illuminated on our panel, "LOW FUEL." Unfortunately, the second approach yielded the same results as the first. Now we both knew that we had made a mistake. We asked the controllers what was the closest airport that was still above visibility minimums. They responded that Lansing, Michigan was still open.

So we headed for Lansing as fast as we could go. Unfortunately, with the type of jet engines that powered this Learjet, we were burning at low altitude about 4 times as much fuel as we burned at cruise altitude. When we arrived at Lansing, we again shot an instrument approach from each of two directions to the minimum altitude, but the fog was already too thick to allow us to see the runway lights. Now we were really low on fuel. We asked the controller what other airport near us was open. He told us Detroit, but added that the visibility was going down fast there, too.

I was now beginning to really fear for my life. As we flew over to Detroit, I was having visions of heaven and talking with the saints of old. I could just see myself conversing with Abraham, Moses, and Peter.

"And how did you die, Peter?" I queried.

"Well," he said, "I was crucified upside-down for the name of Christ. And how did you die, Craig?"

"I was stupid and ran out of fuel in an airplane," I reluctantly had to admit. I really did not want to have that testimony for all of eternity.

When we finally arrived in Detroit, we were the second to the last airplane to make it into the Detroit airport before the fog reduced the visibility below minimums at that airport also. We landed with literally only minutes of fuel left.

One Old, One Young - Blue Flight Suits

Later in July of that year, as I mentioned earlier, I met Jan on the team in Europe. Through the autumn of that year we continued to meet at Jan's parents home every third weekend or so. During this time of getting to know each other, I was relating to Jan the various "heroic" events of my life. One evening at her parents' home, I was sharing with her how I had almost run out of fuel and crashed in a Learjet in Michigan earlier that year. As the story unfolded, a surprised look came upon Jan's face and as I finished, she remarked, "I have to ask you two questions."

"What are those?" I replied.

"Was the other pilot quite a bit older than you?"

"Yes." I replied.

"Were you both wearing light blue, one-piece flight suits?"

"Yes," I replied. "But why would you ask that?"

"We prayed for you!" she announced.

"What do you mean, 'you prayed for me?' This happened in January. I didn't even meet you until July. How could you have prayed for me when you didn't even know me yet?"

Then Jan began to explain. At that time in January 1975, Jan had been part of a YWAM School of Evangelism in Germany. Every morning the students met in small groups for prayer. During the course of their school, a dynamic intercessor and Bible teacher, Joy Dawson, had taught the students a particular prayer model. Usually when people pray, they simply pray for their "shopping list" of all the things that they would like God to help them with. They just pray for the things that are important to them.

In this YWAM school Joy Dawson had taught the students to ask the Lord what was on His heart that day that He would like them to pray. (For more understanding of this method of prayer you may want to listen to the CD teaching entitled, *Why Pray?*[2]) It was their understanding that they were to partner with God in prayer to release His authority on earth to accomplish His purposes.

Consequently, every morning in their small groups the students would first ask the Lord what He wanted for them to pray. They would then share the topics that came to their minds with each other and make a list of these topics. They then proceeded to take each topic one by one and ask the Lord what they were to pray. Frequently, the Holy Spirit would bring to their minds things to pray of which they had no natural cognitive knowledge. Sometimes they would then receive confirmation from natural sources regarding the things that they had prayed, but most times they did not. Each day they were simply faithful to pray what God brought to their minds as a group.

---

[2] Hill, Craig. *Why Pray?* Littleton. Family Foundations International. 2003. CD can be purchased at www.familyfoundations.com

Jan shared with me that one day back in January as they were initially asking the Lord what they were to pray for that day, one of the topics that came up was that they were to pray for an airplane. As they prayed through the list of topics they had for the morning, as was their custom, when they came to the topic "airplane," they naturally asked the Lord, "What are we supposed to pray about an airplane?"

Then one by one each member of the group shared and prayed what came to their minds regarding this topic.

One person said, "I sense that the airplane we are to pray for is very small, but very fast like United" (a U.S. airline company).

Another one contributed, "I sense that there are only two pilots on board. One is old and one is young."

Someone else said, "I see that the two pilots are both wearing light blue one-piece flight suits and they are carrying the U.S. mail."

Jan shared, "I am seeing a map picture of the western part of the Great Lakes area of the United States. The map appears very dark and is growing foggier. I believe the plane is running out of gas, and we need to pray for them to find a place to land."

The group then proceeded to pray for this airplane and for a safe place for it to land. They prayed until they felt like the Holy Spirit had exhausted everything they were to pray for this topic and the job was complete. They then went on to the next topic, which was China, or something that seemed more important in the Kingdom of God.

Jan further related to me that she would not have remembered this specific instance of prayer, as they prayed for things for which they had no natural knowledge every day, so this day was not particularly notable. However, after the prayer time that day, another one of the students who was a member of that small group approached Jan and told her, "Jan, I sense that airplane we prayed for has something to do with you."

Jan thought for a moment and then replied, "I don't really know anyone who is involved with airplanes. I am from small town Iowa. There was a farmer I knew who had a small airplane, which I heard he sometimes flew in and out of his cornfield. But I don't really think it has anything to do with him. I really can't think of anyone else right now."

The other girl in the group said, "Well, I don't know. I just sensed that I was supposed to tell you that."

Jan told me that she wasn't sure what to do with that information, but she trusted the spiritual insights that this girl often got from the Lord. Consequently, she just shelved it in the back of her mind.

As I was sharing my experience, the Holy Spirit brought that incidence of prayer and what the other girl in the group had said back to Jan's remembrance, and that is why she announced to me, "We prayed for you!" We couldn't confirm the exact date, but we knew the prayer and the incident had both taken place in January. We also realized that because of the time zone difference between Germany and Michigan, the time Jan and her group were praying was about the same time that we were having the problem. As Jan shared this incident, I was amazed that God had used the young woman who would be my future wife to pray for me and participate in saving my life six months before we even met.

Hopefully, you can see at this point, that when I viewed life from the perspective that God is in control, there really was very little motivation to pray. The thought was that, "God will simply do what He knows needs to be done, whether I pray or not." However, once I understood prayer from the perspective of an ambassador partnering with God to release His power to accomplish His Kingdom purpose on earth, all of a sudden prayer became much more exciting. The motivation to pray is greatly increased when one realizes that his/her prayers are actually accomplishing something, and that God is hindered from accomplishing His purposes when we don't pray. Everything changes once we understand **that life is not about my trying to get God to listen to me. It is about God's trying to get me to listen to Him.** The issue is not to get God to answer me, but rather to get me to answer God. Life is about my cooperating with Him to get His Kingdom purpose accomplished, not about God cooperating with me to accomplish my selfish purpose. Understanding this may radically change how we pray.

Reflection

1. God combines His power and wisdom with our delegated authority to accomplish His Kingdom purposes on earth.

2. Answered prayer is not so much when God answers us, but rather is when we, as His ambassadors, answer God. After listening to Him, we can then release His power on earth through the authority of the words of our mouths.

3. Intercessory prayer releases God to be impartially partial.

4. When you examine your own prayer life, does it mainly consist of your presenting your "shopping list" to God, or of you listening to God and praying forth that which is on His heart?

5. Are you willing in the future to make yourself available to listen to God and then to pray as His ambassador those things that are on His heart? If so, how much time each week?

Resources

📖 🎧 Two Fleas and No Dog (Book or Audio Book)

🎧   Why Pray? (Single CD Teaching)

chapter 9
SPIRIT AND TRUTH

I have found that in seeking to understand and interpret life's circumstances, there is always a need to balance spiritual and natural truth. Yeshua stated in the passage below, true worshipers must worship the Father in spirit and in truth. I believe that the spirit side refers to the spiritual or unseen realm, while truth refers to the natural or seen realm. Again, life is like a road with two ditches on either side. The enemy seeks to move us off the road into either ditch. Here Yeshua reminds us to stay on the road by worshiping and relating to the Father in both spirit and truth.

But the hour is coming, and now is, when the true worshipers will worship the Father in spirit and truth; for the Father is seeking such to worship Him. God is Spirit, and those who worship Him must worship in spirit and truth." (John 4:23-24)

You may have heard the phrase, "He is so heavenly minded that he is of no earthly good." This defines one ditch, and speaks of a person who has focused on the "spirit" side of life to the exclusion of the natural, or "truth" side. On the other hand, we may meet someone who is so principle oriented that he has no spiritual discernment. Either one of these perspectives is a ditch to be avoided. I make this point here because I believe that many times either God or the devil are blamed for things that in reality are simply the result of human error or natural occurrence. While both God and Satan are indeed involved in human affairs on earth, not everything that happens is a result of the spiritual activity of either God or the kingdom of darkness. Some things are just natural.

If a man does not realize that he must change the oil or add oil to the engine in his car, and consequently runs the car completely out of oil, the engine will probably seize up and be destroyed. Well-meaning "spiritual" friends, depending on whether they see life from either presupposition #1 or #4 may then try to "help" this man interpret this life experience. If the "spiritual" friend sees life from presupposition #1, he may then tell the man that his car engine was destroyed because God was trying to get his attention, humble him, and teach him something. A "spiritual" friend who sees life from presupposition #4 may tell him that the devil was attacking him and trying to steal his finances and hinder his calling. However, could it be that the man simply ran the car out of oil due to lack of knowledge or lack of concern for his car, and his destroyed engine is simply the result of that choice? I think so.

We really want to learn how to live life with a balance between both the spiritual and the natural. I want to operate both within the boundaries of truth and function in spiritual discernment. How would you like to ride in an airliner with a "spirit only" pilot? He tells you that he likes to be led by the Holy Spirit in his piloting.

When you ask him how much the plane can carry, he says, "Oh, it varies. We just load it until we feel by the Spirit that we have the right amount of weight."

When you ask at what speed he lifts off, the pilot tells you, "The copilot and I just pray as we are on takeoff roll on the runway and God gives us a number and we lift off at that speed."

"And at what altitude do you fly?" you ask.

The pilot answers, "We know that the maximum altitude is about forty thousand feet, and the book of Exodus has 40 chapters in it, so usually before takeoff we pray and then just let the Bible fall open to one of the chapters in Exodus. We then use that as our divine guidance in thousands of feet as to what altitude the Lord wants us to cruise at that day. For example, if the Bible falls open to Exodus 31, we cruise at 31,000 feet."

Would you like to ride with that pilot, or would you prefer to fly with a pilot who also knows the principles of aerodynamics, and follows the aircraft manufacturer's recommendations regarding loading and flight dynamics? I would actually like to fly with a pilot who not only understands and abides by the "truth" principles of aerodynamics, but who can also hear from the Holy Spirit while in flight, "Don't fly that route today, but rather take this alternate route. There is unseen danger along the first route." I would like to fly with a pilot like that, who relates to God and to his flying in both spirit and truth, wouldn't you?

Steal, Kill, and Destroy

In understanding natural principles, it should be obvious that both God and Satan use natural principles to impact humanity. It is God's purpose to help man understand natural principles and then use them to benefit mankind. However, it is Satan's purpose to occlude natural principles so that man will violate them to his own detriment. For example, if Satan can keep a man from truly understanding the natural principle of gravity, then it is very likely that such a man will fall or drive off a cliff, and Satan will not have to do anything in order for this man to be destroyed. The man will destroy himself by violating a natural principle. I believe that one of the primary strategies of Satan and the kingdom of darkness is to pervert or hide natural principles of truth. People then violate natural principles due to ignorance or deception and thereby self-destruct. The devil then has very little work to do in his destruction of such people.

In most western nations, if we were to have a call for prayer in almost any congregation, we would find many people requesting prayer. However, the concerns for which 99% of the people request prayer would fall into the same three basic categories:

- Physical Health
- Finances
- Family Relationships.

Someone in the family is facing a major health challenge, and it is not a cold. It is something life-threatening or extremely debilitating such as cancer, heart attack, stroke, diabetes, multiple sclerosis, etc. Others are unemployed, drowning in debt, or are about to lose their house or have a car repossessed. Still others are on the verge of divorce, have adult children in severe marital strife, or are in crisis with a child on drugs or in total rebellion.

If we were to go to the shopping mall and take a survey asking the general public to share with us what are their chief concerns that rob them of inner peace or keep them awake at night, we would find the same three concerns of health, finances, and family relationships. Why is this? Yeshua told us in the Bible that "the thief" uses three natural strategies to accomplish his destructive purposes in our lives.

The thief does not come except to steal, and to kill, and to destroy. I have come that they may have life, and that they may have it more abundantly. (John 10:10)

We see here that these three strategies are to steal, kill, and destroy. One might ask, "Steal what? Kill what? Destroy what?" How about: Steal finances; kill the physical body; destroy marriages and relationships? I believe that this is why we see these same three areas consistently plaguing the lives of so many people. These are the specific areas that Yeshua told us are targeted by the thief. Contrary to this, Yeshua came to bring abundant life into all

> His covenant provisions do not only include eternal life, but also financial life, physical life, and marital, emotional, and relational life.

of these areas. His covenant provisions do not only include eternal life, but also financial life, physical life, and marital, emotional, and relational life.

I believe that a primary strategy of Satan is to deceive people so that they do not understand the truth side of the natural principles that govern these three areas of life. Unknowingly, many people violate these principles and then experience a frustration and lack of understanding as to why, even though they are praying, they are enduring much destruction and adversity in their lives. This is one of the reasons that our ministry, Family Foundations International, has developed weekend seminars in all three of these key areas to help people understand basic life principles and how to practically implement them. We call these basic life principles "ancient paths" from the scripture in Jeremiah 6:16. If you have never attended an Ancient Paths seminar[1], I would highly encourage you to do so at your earliest convenience.

Let's now have a more detailed look at these basic three areas of finances, physical health, and family relationships.

Financial Health (Steal)

If we violate natural financial principles, it is not then a mystery as to how we end up in poverty and slavery. This is not really due to the activity of God or Satan, but rather is the natural fruit of sowing and reaping. A Canadian friend of mine, Earl Pitts, shared with me several years ago a conversation he had with a Jewish accountant. He asked the accountant if he served both Christian and Jewish clients. The accountant said that he did. Earl then asked him which of these two groups of clients did better in business and had stronger financial statements. Laughing, the accountant told him there was no competition. His Jewish clients, of course, were many times more prosperous than his Christian clients.

Earl then asked the accountant why he thought that was. Pausing for a moment, not wanting to offend Earl, the

---

[1] Ancient Paths Seminar: For information on seminars in your local area see our web site at: www.familyfoundations.com

accountant then picked up a Christian Bible lying there on the desk and said something like the following, "I guess it would be for this reason. You Christians tend to live out of the back of the Book. We Jews live out of the front of the Book. Unfortunately for you, most all of the financial principles are in the front of the Book."

Somehow many Christians have thought that they could violate the financial principles in the "Old Testament" Law and that God's "grace" would somehow eliminate the natural consequences of such violation. Unfortunately, as many have discovered, life doesn't work that way. I believe that many Jewish people have prospered for the simple reason that they have adhered to natural financial wisdom expressed in the Biblical Law and Proverbs. However, almost anyone discovering and adhering to these same principles could experience the same beneficial results.

The Debtor Is Slave to the Lender

Let's look at a couple of natural financial principles which seem to be hidden or occluded for many people in our western nations. One key principle is that of financial freedom from debt. Scripture tells us that financial debt creates a master/slave relationship.

The rich rules over the poor, And the borrower is servant to the lender. (Proverbs 22:7)

Several years ago as I was walking into a meeting, I saw a young man wearing a tee shirt on which was printed the message, **"One Master."** Since he was a New Covenant disciple, I assumed that the Master he was speaking of was Yeshua (Jesus Christ). I was to speak on finances that morning, and it suddenly dawned on me that most of the people in the room that day could not legitimately wear that tee shirt because they had credit agreements in writing with many masters. If you carry ongoing financial debt, then you don't have one master, you have multiple masters.

If you don't believe that, try telling your home mortgage or credit card company that for the next year you will not be sending them their regular monthly payment because the LORD has directed you to use that money for a missions project in your congregation. Therefore, you have redirected that money you were sending to that company each month, and it will be unavailable to send them for the next year. Even if you felt that the LORD wanted you to do this, you could not, because you have a prior commitment to other masters to whom you have already designated your monthly cash flow.

If you have taken on personal debt, then you are simply not free to use the resource that God has made available to you as He would direct. You are a slave to your creditors.

In ancient Israel, when it was time to change from a temporary mobile tabernacle to a permanent temple building, the construction was entirely financed through offerings from the congregation. How did they do so? In those times, the people had one master and had not subjected themselves to multiple masters through debt. Each family had authority over their own finances and were thus able to give substantial amounts in offering beyond their tithe. In most congregations today, each family might be directed by the LORD, and might want to give an extra $1000 per month to a missions or building project, but not be able to because each family's monthly cash flow is already committed to many other masters (creditors).

The consequence of this is that since church congregations cannot build a building using the current offerings of the congregants, the church leaders then make the decision to do the same as the congregants. They go to the bank and borrow money to build a building, thus submitting the entire congregation as a servant to a godless master (creditor). Now if the church leaders are asked by the LORD to speak something that may be difficult or unpopular, there is a potential fear in those leaders that many people may leave the church and take their money with them. If this happened, the church couldn't make the monthly payment on the building to the bank, and could potentially lose the building. Through this mechanism, the kingdom of darkness is now able to apply strong pressure on that pastor or leadership team as to what is preached in that congregation. I don't believe that God ever intended for church leadership or individual people to be slaves to multiple credit masters. We should all be able to wear the tee shirt, "One Master."

If the pastor, in his integrity and obedience, does go ahead and preach something controversial or unpopular and people do leave the church, and financial pressure now comes on the church from the bank, people in the congregation may now say, "Oh the devil is attacking our church. He doesn't like what our pastor is preaching." Or they might say, "The devil is using the bank to attack the church." No, the church is just reaping the fruit of the seed of debt. This is just a natural consequence of the master/servant relationship that is created through debt.

How did our entire society end up in a situation in which virtually everyone thinks that personal debt is normal? I would guess that four generations ago no one in our society thought that debt was normal. It would not have even entered into the minds of most of our great grandparents when they were young to borrow money for thirty or forty years in order to buy a house. Today in the United States, most young married couples would not think it possible to own a house without incurring debt. Yet our grandparents all had houses. How did they do it?

Four generations ago there was still a concept of generational blessing operative in families. Parents and grandparents expected to make some resources available to help their children. So family members would help purchase materials, and the extended family, or sometimes the entire community, would come together and help build the new couple a house. Today, many families have abandoned any concept of generational blessing. To learn how to eliminate your debt and ensure that your children and grandchildren will never incur any debt, see my DVD series, *The GOOD Plan*[2].

I believe that there probably has been a purposeful strategy in the kingdom of darkness over the last four generations to introduce the concept of debt into our society on a wholesale basis. Through this mechanism, Satan has been able to get the vast majority of the population to voluntarily submit themselves as servants to individuals and institutions already controlled by the kingdom of darkness.

Jubilee Is Coming

For the last decade as I have ministered in various congregations across North America and in other nations, I

---

[2] Hill, Craig. *The GOOD Plan DVD Series*. Littleton: Family Foundations International, 2006.

have asked people if the LORD has been speaking anything in the congregation prophetically about finances. Consistently, congregational leaders have told me that they have heard from the LORD the word, "Get out of debt." I think that there is another reason other than not being a servant to multiple masters that the LORD has been telling the body of Messiah for several years to get out of debt. It has to do with the times in which we live.

Everything in nature experiences cycles. Seasons, your marriage, your body, churches, businesses, and national economies all go through cycles. They all go up and down and up again. If people have no recognition of where they are in a particular cycle, and fail to prepare for the next season or phase of a cycle, they are then caught unaware and again ascribe to God or Satan the natural consequences of their ignorance and choices.

God prescribed in ancient Israel the economic practice of purging the economy of all debt every fifty years. This practice was known as "Jubilee." Whenever credit is made available to people in a society, human nature dictates that people will always borrow to excess. They will borrow beyond their capability to repay. For this reason, God prescribed the Jubilee in Israel to normalize and reset the economy every fifty years. If one knows exactly when Jubilee is coming, then no one is surprised or hurt when it occurs. Everyone structures their loans based upon a known date of the forgiveness of all debts. Unfortunately, it is not possible to perpetuate a market economy without periodic times of purging excess debt (Jubilee). If a government will not plan for Jubilee, then unfortunately that economy will experience unplanned times of Jubilee.

The last major Jubilee time in which we experienced a major debt purge in America was in 1929 and continuing through the decade of the 1930s. We now call that time "The Great Depression." Excess debt was purged through bankruptcy and many families lost all of their financial assets. Banks were closed, and businesses shut down as a result of people being blindsided, having no idea that it was Jubilee (debt purge) time.

We have not really had another significant purging of debt in the U.S. since the 1930s. I believe that we are now overdue for another Jubilee time of purging debt. I am writing this chapter in the early part of 2008. Already in this year we are seeing a huge decline in our U.S. housing market, and even the talking heads on the TV financial news shows are beginning to use the "R" word—recession. Just this week, the U.S. stock market index dropped 500 points in one day and the U.S. Federal Reserve bank immediately dropped interest rates ¾ of a point.

I am convinced that we are headed very soon for the type of economic slowdown (depression) that accompanies unplanned Jubilees. It seems that many people, even economists, have not understood the fact that in any market economy, you do not get a choice of whether a Jubilee debt purge comes or not. One only gets a choice as to whether one plans and prepares for it or not.

Now, who is potentially harmed in an unplanned debt purge (recession/depression)? Primarily the people who are in debt and did not recognize that a recession/depression was coming. Many such people may see the value of their house sink to be significantly less than the mortgaged amount still owed to the bank. Some of them may also lose their jobs or businesses. Can you now see why the Spirit of God might have been saying prophetically to the body of Messiah for the last ten years, "Get out of debt?" Unfortunately, in my experience to this point, very few people have actually heeded this word and eliminated their debt.

The Meek Shall Inherit the Earth

Several years ago, I got a new understanding of the well-known Bible verse from Matthew 5:5 in which Yeshua stated, *"Blessed are the meek, for they shall inherit the earth."* Most people know that meek does not mean weak. But what exactly does it mean? In study of this, I ran across a definition of the word "meek" that really brought a whole new meaning to this passage. Years ago I ran across a very pertinent definition of the word, meek. I no longer have record of the original source in order to give proper credit. I do believe, however, that this definition gives an accurate description of a critical aspect of the meaning of this word. **Meekness is having great power or resource and using only a percentage of it.**

So by this definition, to be meek is to live on 60%, 70% or 80% of available resource. This is talking about having margins in your life. Not living life to the edge of the page. Now this is really anti-cultural at this time in America. So if meekness is having great resource or power and using less than 100% of it, then what would the opposite be? It would be having limited resource or power and using more than 100% of it. We have one word that describes this situation. It is called "debt." I suddenly realized that **debt and meekness are opposites.** Now, Yeshua said that two things would happen to meek people:

1) They would be blessed; and
2) They would inherit the earth.

I discovered that the Greek word translated here as "earth" really would be better translated as "land." So the meek will inherit the land. Suddenly I saw the very practical application of this verse here and now. I remembered hearing many people my parents' age who had lived through the last Jubilee in the 1930s say things like, "My father lost his house in the depression," or "My uncle lost his farm," or "My friend lost his business."

If someone lost possession of a house, farm, or business in the depression time, then someone else must have gained possession of it. Now, who lost the possessions and why? The people who lost houses, lands, farms, and businesses were the people who were indebted and lost these things because they couldn't pay for them. Usually the bank then repossessed the property and sold it at auction for pennies on the dollar.

So who gained possession of these things? The people with a little bit of extra cash. What are these people called? Meek! I suddenly saw that in the last debt purge, the meek inherited the land, while the indebted lost the land. I then understood this principle: Whenever economic shaking comes to any economy resulting in a purge of excess debt, there is always a large transfer of wealth. The wealth, however, transfers from the indebted to the meek. In this way, Matthew 5:5 is fulfilled in a very practical sense. The indebted are not blessed and lose the land, while the meek are blessed and inherit the land.

I have heard many people talk about the coming wealth transfer and they quote, "The wealth of the wicked is laid up for the righteous." The problem is that many did not stop to check to see who "the wicked" might be. Psalm 37:21 advises us of one category of "wicked."

The wicked borrows and does not repay, but the righteous shows mercy and gives. (Psalm 37:21)

208

I believe that we are headed for a huge wealth transfer beginning very soon. This is why the Spirit of God has instructed those with ears to hear to get out of debt, so that they will not be the ones from whom, but rather be the ones to whom, the wealth is transferring. In this way, meek people will be positioned to be "the righteous" who can show mercy and give.

Jan and I felt compelled by the Spirit of God back in 1995 to aggressively move to eliminate all debt in our lives. As we took natural steps to do so, we found that God took supernatural steps on our behalf. Consequently, we made our last mortgage payment (which was our only debt) in early 2002. Since that time, we have been able to wear the tee shirt with integrity that says, "One Master!" If you are still under financial pressure and have not yet eliminated all personal debt, I would highly recommend you attend an Ancient Paths Seminar: Financial Foundations[3] at your earliest convenience.

As this next debt purge cycle ensues in our economy, again those who have understood the times and prepared will not experience excessive financial pressure in their lives. However, those who have not understood natural economic cycles (Truth side) or heeded the voice of the Spirit of God (Spirit side) may find themselves under enormous financial pressure and stress. There may be a tendency to blame God or think that this is an attack of the devil on their lives. In reality, this is simply the natural consequence of violating a

[3] Ancient Paths Seminar: Financial Foundations. Littleton: Family Foundations International. 2008. www.familyfoundations.com

basic financial principle and becoming the personal servant of an earthly master (creditor), rather than having only One Master.

Physical Health (Kill)

The second area in which the enemy uses ignorance and the violation of natural principles to destroy is in the arena of physical health. In this realm, again, many people perceive a spiritual attack of the enemy when they are primarily experiencing the simple consequences of the violation of natural law.

We spoke earlier in this chapter about vital financial principles that are contained in "the front of the Book," that are significantly ignored or "written off" by many New Covenant disciples. Similarly, two other vital principles which seem to be ignored pertain to the support and maintenance of physical health. These were designed by God to counteract the thief's "kill" strategy. These two principles are those pertaining to clean and unclean foods, and honoring the Sabbath.

Clean Food and Sabbath Rest Reduce Stress

God outlined in His word for His people foods that are "clean" and should be eaten, and foods that are "unclean" and should not be eaten (Deuteronomy 14). Again, I am convinced that there is a reason why God said this, and that indeed this instruction given to the Hebrew people through Moses was not just for Jewish people in past times, but rather expressed a wise protective boundary for all people. When these dietary principles are violated, I believe we may subject ourselves to natural consequences that we don't yet understand. God, however, knew these things and therefore gave us this instruction. This may be an area you may want to study for yourself for more understanding.[4]

As we discussed in the realm of finances, the principle of living a meek lifestyle also applies to our physical bodies. Here in the United States, as in most western countries, we live in a culture of debt in most aspects of life. Not only do many people live in financial debt, but they also live in the realm of debt in their usage of time, energy, and relationships. Many people overbook their day just like the airlines, hoping at least one appointment will cancel so that they can make it through the day. We have no distinction of days between "holy" and "common," so everything runs 24/7.

Again, God gave us a prescription in the front of "The Book" designed to help us establish a lifestyle of meekness, particularly regarding the usage of our time. This principle is that of remembering and honoring God's Sabbath (Shabbat in Hebrew). Honoring Shabbat was apparently so important to God that He actually included this in the "Ten Commandments" (Exodus 20:8-11). The Shabbat was designed to create time, energy and relational margins for God's people. He designed us to set boundaries for our time usage and to live in meekness, resting our bodies, minds, and emotions one complete day in each seven. When we refuse to honor His Shabbat, we violate both a spiritual and natural principle, and place ourselves under a level of stress that God

---

[4] Townsley, Cheryl, N.D. *The Power of Being Healthy*. Littleton: Lifestyle for Health: 2006. www.familyfoundations.com

never intended for anyone to endure. The results of this violation are not a mystery, but are really quite predictable.

A lack of meekness in time (not honoring Shabbat) and money (personal debt) results in lack of meekness in relationships and physical energy. Violation of these basic biblical principles results in increased levels of STRESS. Prolonged periods of living under high levels of stress can easily take a long-term toll on the physical body's capacity to function normally. Then, when various systems in the body begin to malfunction, many people still refuse to adjust their lifestyle, but rather consider this a spiritual attack of the enemy and potentially exacerbate the problem through the regular ingestion of over-the-counter or prescribed toxic chemical poisons (pharmaceutical drugs).

If we were to look at the major life threatening challenges to health that many people in our western countries face today, it is amazing to recognize that virtually none of them are diseases resulting from viral or bacterial threat from the outside. Neither are they just symptoms of growing old. The types of challenges people face today are cancer, heart disease, diabetes, stroke, multiple sclerosis, chronic fatigue syndrome, fibromyalgia, rheumatoid arthritis, etc. Again, none of these are contagious, nor are they symptoms of growing old. Every one of these challenges is a result of the malfunction of some bodily system, many of them being related to immune system malfunction.

If we compare the incidence of these health challenges today with the health challenges facing people one hundred years ago, we would find that the incidence of these types of chronic degenerative malfunctions was almost not known amongst our population. Most of the health challenges one hundred years ago were contagious diseases such as smallpox, polio, tuberculosis, yellow fever, influenza, etc. So what has

212

changed in the last one hundred years that has given rise to our own bodies' destroying themselves from the inside out?

I believe that there are three primary changes:

1. Depletion of nutritional content of food due to green harvesting, mass production, and processing.

2. Unavoidable, continual intake of man-made toxic chemicals (in small quantities) through food, air and water. (I am told that there are over 400 different toxic chemicals now found in small amounts in the blood of every American that did not even exist before World War II.)

3. Lack of financial, relational, and time margins (meekness) has produced an increased emotional stress level under which we live today that is unheard of in past history.

The advent of the three issues listed above is no doubt a long-term strategy of the kingdom of darkness to kill our physical bodies and take us out of our God-given destinies at an early age. However, when someone is afflicted with one or more of the above-mentioned types of chronic degenerative conditions, not in every case, but in many cases, this is really the result of lack of knowledge and poor stewardship of the physical body, not a specific attack of the enemy on that person at that time. This effective longer-term strategy of the enemy is to keep us corporately ignorant of how to care for our physical bodies, in which case we will self-destruct, and he won't have to waste his time or energy specifically attacking us at all.

For Lack of Knowledge My People Perish

Over the years, I have observed the incredible difference that lifestyle changes and nutritional support have made in the lives of my own family members and friends. This has confirmed to me that many people are unknowingly violating natural laws regarding the maintenance of their physical bodies, and are perishing as a result of that lack of knowledge. Others are gaining the necessary knowledge and thus are prolonging their lives in increased quality. Let me contrast below two women I have known who recently faced the challenge of breast cancer. The first one is my mother, Vonnie Hill, now in her eighties. My father wrote the following account in an annual family newsletter in 2005.

"Our battle against cancer started 5 years ago (i.e., December, 2000) when Vonnie was first diagnosed with breast cancer. In January, 2001, Vonnie had lumpectomy surgery to remove the cancerous tumor. This started our study of cancer and the health-maintenance capability of God's 'intelligent design' for the human body to heal itself of all degenerative diseases, including cancer.

Based on our early studies of this subject, we rejected consideration of the traditional medical/pharmaceutical therapies of radiation and chemotherapy and focused on a 'wellness program' of building up our immune systems for bodily self-healing.

Unfortunately, we were a little too slow and too late in learning about and implementing this God-provided, natural-self-healing 'wellness program.' Consequently, Vonnie's cancerous tumor started growing again, resulting in further diagnosis in early 2004 of tumor growth in the same breast at the site of the prior lumpectomy surgery. By this time we had learned about nature-based, immune-building therapies. In

November of 2004, Vonnie and I scheduled a three-week natural therapy session at [specific treatment center].

After these three weeks Vonnie's cancerous tumor shrank by 25% in size, and all blood-analysis markers showed no signs of cancer. The hospital staff then prescribed a home-therapy program, which we continued to follow for the next four months. In March, 2005, we returned to the [specific treatment center] for a checkup. The hospital staff reported the tumor had further shrunk to about 50% of original size, and all blood markers showed no cancer activity. A subsequent CAT scan showed Vonnie's breast tumor totally inactive with no sign of life.

Presently, we are here at [specific treatment center] for our one-year checkup and a progress evaluation for the elimination of Vonnie's tumor and cancer. Thankfully, the current report again confirms continuing reduction in Vonnie's tumor size and no indication of cancer from the blood-analysis markers. Throughout this therapy program, Vonnie has suffered no pain and has been able to live a normal, active, pain-free life."

Up until the present time there has been no recurrence of my mom's cancer and the tumor has continued to shrink in size. Please understand that I am in no way suggesting that you or anyone you know should disregard the opinion or counsel of your doctor or medical professional. If you are facing a serious health challenge, please listen to the counsel of your doctor or health professional, but also pray to get God's wisdom, and educate yourself as to the function of your own body. In this way you will be able to make a wise decision considering all natural and spiritual knowledge available to you.

I would like to contrast this experience of my mom's with that of a friend of ours, about twenty years younger than my mom, who also discovered a cancerous lump in her breast at about the same time as Mom did.

Unfortunately, our friend did not have the same understanding of how to support the body's own ability to keep itself healthy. Consequently, she did not make lifestyle changes, pursue natural therapies, or add nutritional support to her diet. Being a strong covenant believer in the LORD, however, she continued to pray, confess scripture over her body, and claim her healing. The cancer, however, continued to spread. After spiritually battling the cancer for about a year and a half, our friend finally submitted her body to chemotherapy. We attended her funeral about two years after she had discovered the lump.

In attempting to interpret this circumstance, we would have to ask, what was the difference between our friend and my mom? They were both strong New Covenant disciples. They both knew the covenant provisions regarding healing, and prayed accordingly. Same God, same covenant, same blood of Messiah. What was the difference? One gained knowledge of what was needed to support the natural defense systems designed by God to keep the body healthy, while the other rejected that knowledge as not being pertinent. In my opinion, our friend only worshipped the Father and lived her life in spirit, but not in truth. My mom, on the other hand, worships and is living in both spirit and truth. Unfortunately in this case, for lack of natural knowledge, our friend perished (Hosea 4:6).

Many people like our friend, who have not educated themselves as to the lifestyle and nutritional support required by the body for normal function, become very confused spiritually when their body systems malfunction, resulting in some sort of self-destructive, chronic, degenerative condition. I have heard of several people who have been supernaturally healed of cancer or another terminal condition, only to die of that same condition a few years later. Believing friends and relatives around such a person, still not understanding natural principles, attempt to find a spiritual reason as to why this happened. Many times the answer is simply the violation of natural principles pertaining to the support of bodily systems.

I have likened this situation to an owner running a car out of oil without knowledge that the car needs oil in order for its lubrication system to function normally. When the engine seizes up and stops running, being a spiritual person, the owner prays to God for a miracle. Suppose that God does indeed perform a miracle and supernaturally restores the engine to working condition and replenishes the crankcase with oil. The "spiritual" owner is overjoyed and testifies of this miracle to many others.

However, suppose that the owner still does not receive the knowledge of the need to change or replenish the oil in the car's lubrication system. Consequently, a couple of years later, the car runs out of oil again, and once again the engine is destroyed and stops working. The owner is now spiritually confused and once again begins praying for the supernatural intervention of God to restore the engine. Perhaps other well meaning friends now tell this owner that he lost his "healing" in his car because of unbelief, or sin, or lack of diligence in seeking God, or many other "spiritual" reasons. It doesn't dawn on the owner the reason could be as simple as having run the car out of oil again. Not understanding this natural principle causes much confusion, as this owner and his "spiritual" friends seek to understand theologically why God would "allow" his car engine to be destroyed again. Thus John 4:23 applies: Spirit AND Truth.

Can God supernaturally restore the car engine? Of course He can. He did this already once. However, is this the normal way that God intends for people to live? No, of course not. It is His intention for people to obtain the knowledge of how to properly care for and maintain their car. It is not God's plan for people to rely upon supernatural miracles while refusing to provide their cars with the necessary fluid support and maintenance. I believe that the same is true regarding our physical bodies. A friend of ours, Dr. Cheryl Townsley, who is a naturopathic doctor, has created a wonderful DVD teaching series with very simple layman's explanation of some lifestyle changes and ways you could begin to more effectively maintain and support the systems of your physical body. This DVD teaching series is called *The Power of Being Healthy*,[5] and can be ordered from our Family Foundations website.

Free to Run Again

I would like to share with you a personal story regarding the potential destruction from the lack of knowledge of proper natural maintenance and support of bodily systems. My wife, Jan, has a cousin, Barb, whom we have not visited much or known well. However, we have known that she is a strong New Covenant disciple who loves the LORD. In January of 2005, we received Barb's annual family newsletter in which she shared with us that she had been engaged in a serious battle with multiple sclerosis. Barb was requesting prayer in that the MS was really taking a toll on her ability to function as a mom and wife in her family.

---

[5] Townsley, Cheryl, N.D. *The Power of Being Healthy*. Littleton: Lifestyle for Health: 2006. www.familyfoundations.com

She reported that already she barely had enough energy daily to perform the necessary functions around the house. She would get up and fix breakfast, get her husband off to work and her kids off to school. Then she would go back to bed until mid afternoon, at which time she would get up, attempt to do a little housework and prepare her family an evening meal. After cleaning up from dinner, Barb would then go to bed about eight or eight-thirty. That was her day every day. She also reported to us that she could only walk three to five blocks total in the course of a day before becoming totally exhausted. As Jan and I read this letter, our hearts broke for Barb and we prayed for her. However, we had enough knowledge by that time to realize that these symptoms Barb was experiencing were not just the result of a spiritual attack against her destiny as a wife and mother, but were probably also a result of serious nutritional deficiency. Apparently, her own immune system had been attacking and destroying the mylon sheath around her nerves. We knew that God did not design the immune system to attack the nervous system, but rather to support and defend it. Due to our experience with others, it seemed to us that Barb's body was literally being starved of some vital nutrients used by the body to help facilitate normal, healthy immune system function, and she simply didn't know it.

After praying, Jan and I felt that the LORD wanted us to purchase a particular nutritional supplement for Barb containing key nutrients in which we believed her body was deficient. We called and asked her if she would diligently consume the supplement if we provided it to her, which she agreed to do. About six weeks later, we received an e-mail form Barb sharing with us what had happened. Following are portions from this e-mail.

"Hi Jan,

I hope you guys had a wonderful trip to Brazil. [My husband] and I just got back from a wonderful week in NYC. (I took my [supplements] with me.) Neither of us had been there before and [my husband] had business, so I went along.

I don't even know what to say to you to express my gratitude right now. I wake up every day with complete joy in my heart and praising God and you guys. I'm a completely different person from where I was 6 weeks ago. I don't even know why I deserve this blessing from God, through you guys, of good health - it's very humbling and brings me to tears often. I don't even know how to live like this after years of having to think about my limitations caused by my MS and how much I could get done in a day. My thinking has had to change daily about what my life is now - with good health. I'll lay in bed early in the morning thinking I should try to go back to sleep so I'll have enough energy to get up and 'go' - and then I think, 'no, I don't need more sleep because I feel great.'

The trip to NYC was nothing less than a miracle and [my husband] and I just couldn't get over how well I did and how much I was able to do. I walked between 3-5 miles each day - when a couple months ago I could only walk a couple blocks. In the airports, [my husband] would be looking for a cart to drive me to the next gate and I'd say, 'remember, I don't need one anymore.' It just was a wonderful, miraculous trip! I have had to carry a pillow around with me because if I sit on a chair that's too hard for more than 10 minutes, my legs would be completely numb and it was difficult to walk. In NYC, I sat for 1 1/2 hours on a hard bench at a restaurant with only a little tingling in my feet.

I've said for a couple years now that a great desire of mine was to be able to walk as far as I could see - as in I'd see something a distance away that I'd like to see up close, but knew I couldn't get there. And now I can! I'm not taking this good health for granted and know it may not last forever - so am enjoying each day as the Lord gives it to me. It is making such a difference in my whole life and that of my family. I really have very little of my MS symptoms left at this point and am starting to tell friends and relatives about my newfound health, how I got it, etc and giving all the praise and glory to God. I hadn't been telling anyone before now, because I really didn't know what to make of it or if it was real. Everyone is so thrilled for me, even my friends and relatives who are much more sick than I am....

Anyway, I just couldn't go another day without letting you know my terrific progress and how grateful I am for you!

Thank you from the bottom of my heart and God bless you!

Love, Barb"

This letter was written now about two years ago. Barb's physical health is not without challenges, but overall has continued to improve. Two and a half years ago, Barb could not even imagine that she would ever have the energy to serve her family as she desired. She is now full of life and has the energy to be able to do everything necessary for her household. She even has the extra energy to care for her niece's baby two days every other week. I share this with you here as an example of the critical need to understand and interpret life experience not just from the spiritual standpoint, but also from the natural. Had no one realized what Barb was experiencing was simply her own body's natural response to being deprived of vital nutrients (starvation, or similar to running the car out of oil), her physical condition may have become significantly worse for no reason other than lack of knowledge (Hosea 4:6). We realized that her symptoms were not the result of a "mysterious" spiritual attack of the enemy, nor of "God trying to punish her or get her attention." Again, in this case it was critical to live in both spirit and truth (John 4:23).

Family Relationships (Destroy)

The third area in which the enemy seeks to keep us ignorant of natural principles is in the area of family relationships. Again, the primary strategy of Satan and the kingdom of darkness is to keep us ignorant of long-term sowing and reaping cycles. In ministering to people, I have found that certain people are strongly affected by generational patterns and cycles, of which they are totally unaware. Some people have a generational pattern of divorce and remarriage that creates challenges for them in marriage which others don't face who don't have such a cycle operative. Sometimes choices are made in life to violate basic principles of marriage and family that result in natural consequences for multiple generations. When we experience these struggles in relationships, many times such struggles are not a result of the specific activity of God at that time, nor are they the result of an attack from the kingdom of darkness. This is just the result again of the violation of natural principles.

Noel and Phyl Gibson in their book *Evicting Demonic Squatters and Breaking Bondages*[6] quote some very interesting statistics traced over two hundred years pertaining to two American families.

"Max Jukes was an atheist who married a godless woman. Some 560 descendants were traced:

310 died as paupers, 150 became criminals, 7 of them murderers, 100 were known drunkards, and half the

---

[6] Gibson, Noel and Phyl. *Evicting Demonic Squatters and Breaking Bondages*. Drummeyne: Freedom in Christ Ministries Trust. 1987

women were prostitutes. The descendants of Max Jukes cost the United States government more than 1.25 million dollars in 19th century dollars.

Jonathan Edwards was a contemporary of Max Jukes. He was a committed Christian who gave God first place in his life. He married a godly young lady, and some 1,394 descendants were traced:

295 graduated from college, of whom 13 became college presidents, and 65 became professors, 3 were elected as United States Senators, 3 as state governors, and others were sent as ministers to foreign countries, 30 were judges, 100 were lawyers, one the dean of an outstanding law school, 56 practiced as physicians, one was the dean of a medical school, 75 became officers in the military, 100 were well-known missionaries, preachers and prominent authors, another 80 held some form of public office, of whom 3 were mayors of large cities, 1 was the Comptroller of the U.S. Treasury, and another was vice president of the United States."

It is amazing to observe that not one of the descendants of the Edwards family was ever a liability to the government. In understanding the natural consequences of choices made within these two family lineages, we see that if you would have been born into the Jukes family, you would probably have had a much more difficult time in mar-

> God has picked you out in this generation to make wise, godly choices that will make marriage and family relationships easier for your children and future generations.

riage and raising children than if you had been born into the Edwards family. However, no matter which type of family background you come from, the very fact that you are reading this book is probably strong evidence that God has picked you out in this generation to make wise, godly choices that will make marriage and family relationships easier for your children and future generations. In any generation it is possible to recognize and break the power of negative generational patterns and initiate new godly generational patterns. We have seen this happen for many individuals and families in a very dramatic way as they have attended a Family Foundations Ancient Paths Seminar[7].

In ministering to people I have found that many people have not recognized the devastating natural and spiritual consequences of sexual immorality. Certainly most people understand the threat of unwanted pregnancies and sexually transmitted diseases. However, many people have not understood the seed that is potentially sown into children for generations. We find in scripture a principle that iniquity has the potential to pass generationally for at least three to four generations (Exodus 20:5).

King David and his family lineage provide a good example from scripture of this principle. David had no idea of the ultimate cost to his family and to the kingdom of Israel of his sin of adultery. We find in 2 Samuel 11 that at a time when King David should have been out at battle with his troops, he was at home in the palace, bored. His eyes wandered in a direction they should not have, and David purposefully committed the sin of adultery with Bathsheba. To cover his sin, he then had her husband, Uriah, murdered, and then

---

[7] For more information on Ancient Paths Seminars see the Family Foundations International website at www.familyfoundations.com

224

took Bathsheba to be his wife. We read in Psalm 51 of David's confession and repentance.

Have mercy upon me, O God, according to Your lovingkindness; according to the multitude of Your tender mercies, blot out my transgressions. Wash me thoroughly from my iniquity, and cleanse me from my sin. For I acknowledge my transgressions, and my sin is always before me. (Psalm 51:1-3)

We find that even though David had a contrite and repentant heart, and God forgave David of his sins and iniquity, there was still a natural sowing and reaping consequence that affected his family. First we find in 2 Samuel 12 this first child conceived by David and Bathsheba died. Without realizing it, through his sin David released a generational iniquity of sexual immorality, murder and death into the lives of his children. In chapter 13 we find one of David's sons, Amnon, raping his sister Tamar. Tamar's brother, Absalom, is so angered by Amnon's violation of his sister that Absalom kills his brother Amnon. Now we have the fruit of death, sexual immorality and murder already manifest in the second generation of David's progeny. Absalom then enters into rebellion and insurrection against his father, David, and his rulership.

Subsequently, we find David's best friend and trusted counselor, Ahithophel, turning against David and siding with Absalom. When Absalom's army drives David and his army out of Jerusalem, Ahithophel counsels Absalom to publicly humiliate his father, King David, by sexually defiling his father's concubines in a tent pitched on the palace roof (2 Samuel 16:20-23). Absalom indeed then does so. It is extremely interesting to discover further information on the identity of this trusted counselor, Ahithophel. Not only was he King David's best friend and trusted counselor, but he also happened to be Bathsheba's grandfather (2 Samuel 23:34; 2 Samuel 11:3). All those years since David first committed adultery with Bathsheba and killed her husband, Ahithophel must have carried bitterness in his heart, waiting for this opportunity to take his revenge on David. Here we have a further unseen relational consequence of David's sin against Bathsheba and Uriah.

In looking to interpret this set of circumstances, David could have simply thought that this was God's dealing with him or was an attack of Satan and the kingdom of darkness. However, these events in his family were really just the natural fruit of the prior seed of immorality and murder sown by David. Later in chapter 18 of Second Samuel, we find that David's son, Absalom, was killed in the civil war. Overall, David lost three sons to death and bore the devastation of his own daughter and concubines being sexually defiled by his own sons.

Subsequently, we find that this same seed of immorality and lust pervaded David's family lineage. His son, Solomon, who reigned after David's death, although known for his great wisdom, was satisfied with no less than 1,000 women with whom to fulfill his lust (1 Kings 11:3). As we follow the lineage of Solomon's sons, we find that his son, Rehoboam, in his foolishness splits the kingdom, and there is a perpetuation of idolatry, murder and immorality among the Hebrew kings for many multiple generations. In the end, we see that neither David's contrite heart, nor his confession and repentance stopped the natural consequences emanating from the seed of his adultery and murder.

The good news for us today is that we have a much more potent covenant with God than did King David. The blood of Yeshua Ha Meshiach (Jesus Christ) was shed not only to create a way to forgive us of our sins, but also to break the power of generational iniquity and sinful patterns.

Let me share with you a modern day example of this. Paul and Sally (not their real names) met each other when Paul was in a private school and Sally was working by serving food in the school cafeteria. Quickly falling in love with each other, this young couple soon found themselves involved sexually, and Sally became pregnant out of wedlock at age 17. Without realizing it, Paul and Sally had released a seed of immorality into the life of their daughter. This iniquity then opened a spiritual door for the same sin to be repeated in future generations. Not knowing this, Paul and Sally married and later both became committed New Covenant disciples of Yeshua. They confessed and repented of their own pre-marital sexual immorality, but did not realize that an active seed of immorality was still operative in their daughter, Cindy (not her real name). Much to their dismay, at age 17 Cindy repeated the pattern of her parents, also fell into sexual immorality and became pregnant. She later married and subsequently became a committed disciple of Yeshua.

However, unbeknownst to Paul, Sally or Cindy, the seed of immorality was still active in the family. The next fruit of this seed was even more devastating. Cindy's four-year-old little boy, Kyle, was sexually molested by an older adult at a preschool. Paul and Sally were beside themselves with grief over what had happened to their little grandson. Paul was so filled with anger that everything within him wanted to kill the perpetrator of this injustice against his grandson.

Fortunately, within the next year, Paul and Sally attended an Ancient Paths Seminar[8]. At this seminar they learned about the potential generational consequences of opening the door to sexual immorality. They also learned that they had authority in Messiah to close this door in the spirit realm and to expel the seed of immorality from their family by the blood of Yeshua. With this new understanding, Paul and Sally used their authority in Messiah to close the door to this iniquity and expel the seed of immorality in their family, thereby terminating the natural sowing and reaping consequences of this seed for future generations.

Now many years have passed and it is evident that this seed of immorality and family destruction was removed as Kyle, Paul and Sally's grandson, who is now twenty years old, has not repeated the pattern of his mother and grandparents becoming involved in sexual immorality and an unplanned pregnancy at age seventeen. Kyle is a godly young man who is committed to remain sexually pure for his wife. Thus, the good news is that no matter what doors of generational iniquity we may have opened or seeds of destruction we might have sown, the blood of Messiah is always available to us in covenant to remove that seed and close the opened spiritual doors.

In conclusion, we see the critical need to learn to live our lives in both spirit and truth. Not everything that happens to us has a short-term spiritual origin. Many destructive circumstances in our lives are truly the result of our willful or ignorant violation of natural principles. Thus, in

[8] Ancient Paths Seminar, For more information, see: www.familyfoundations.com

interpreting the circumstances of life, we must always remember to ask God if there are natural principles that we have violated which we can learn and set aright. In this way, we can remain on the balanced road of spirit and truth without falling off into the ditch on either side.

Reflection

1. In understanding life's circumstances, we must always balance the spirit (faith) side with the truth (natural) side of life.

2. The enemy consistently utilizes three strategies to take us out of our destinies: Steal, Kill, and Destroy (John 10:10). Attack against finances, health and relationships.

3. Personal debt is one strategy of the enemy to financially enslave people to himself.

4. Debt and meekness are opposites. Meekness means having margins in life.

5. There is a large transfer of wealth coming from the indebted to the meek.

6. We have depleted the nutrient value of our food, and have created a toxic, chemicalized, high-stress environment.

7. We are now experiencing a world-wide crisis in personal physical health as a result of lack of knowledge of the above problems.

8. We are also experiencing moral and relational crises resulting in generational cycles of marriage and family breakdown.

9. In which area do you most need support and help: Finances, Physical Health, or Family Relationships?

10. Do you find that you are more unbalanced on the truth (natural/principle) side, or on the spirit (faith) side in living your life?

11. In what aspects of your life have you ascribed to God or the devil events that were simply the natural consequences of life?

Resources

[1] The Ancient Paths Seminar: See the Appendix for details and www.familyfoundations.com for a schedule of upcoming events.

[1] An Ancient Paths Seminar: Financial Foundations: See the Appendix for details and www.familyfoundations.com for a schedule of upcoming events.

(•) The GOOD Plan (DVDs with computer CD providing computer spreadsheet debt reduction tool and instructions)

(•) The Power of Being Healthy, Cheryl Townsley, N.D. (DVDs with computer CD including handout documents)

📖 *Wealth, Riches & Money*

chapter 10
HOW TO VIEW
SUFFERING AND
ADVERSITY

Apostle Peter tells us that it is inevitable that we will suffer injustice in this life. Not only that, he tells us that we were called to suffer injustice at the hands of evil men. This is not a surprise once we understand that we are ambassadors of a government (Kingdom of God) that is hated, and against which war is being made on earth. Peter tells us the following:

For what credit is it if, when you are beaten for your faults, you take it patiently? But when you do good and suffer, if you take it patiently, this is commendable before God. For to this you were called, because Christ also suffered for us leaving us an example, that you should follow His steps: "Who committed no sin, nor was deceit found in His mouth"; who, when He was reviled, did not revile in return; when He suffered, He did not threaten, but committed Himself to Him who judges righteously; who Himself bore our sins in His own body on the tree, that we, having died to sins, might live for righteousness—by whose stripes you were healed. (1 Peter 2:20-24)

We see from this scripture passage that it is inevitable we will experience injustice and evil, just as did Yeshua, the One we follow. However, we also see that Peter understands the power of the healing purchased for us by the blood of Yeshua. He quotes in this passage the New Covenant promise of healing from Isaiah 53, but does not apply it here to sickness. The healing Peter is referring to in this passage is necessary as a result of being beaten, abused or unjustly treated by people. Yeshua was unjustly beaten on our behalf to purchase the healing for us that may be necessary as a result of our being beaten, abused or unjustly treated.

I really believe that Apostle Paul had a revelation (true bicycle knowledge) of this provision of the covenant better than just about anyone. In the passage below he describes some of the difficulties he was facing.

But we have this treasure in earthen vessels, that the excellence of the power may be of God and not of us. We are hard-pressed on every side, yet not crushed; we are perplexed, but not in despair; persecuted, but not forsaken; struck down, but not destroyed—always carrying about in the body the dying of the Lord Jesus, that the life of Jesus also may be manifested in our body. For we who live are always delivered to death for Jesus' sake, that the life of Jesus also may be manifested in our mortal flesh. So then death is working in us, but life in you. (2 Corinthians 4:7-12)

We see here that Paul understood the battle, his ambassadorship, and the promises of his covenant with God. While he was not surprised by the difficulties presented by people and his life's circumstances, Paul also did not ascribe the works of the devil to God. Paul experienced some pretty significant suffering, evil and injustice, yet he called all of it "momentary light affliction."

Therefore we do not lose heart. Even though our outward man is perishing, yet the inward man is being renewed day by day. For our light affliction, which is but for a moment, is working for us a far more exceeding and eternal weight of glory, while we do not look at the things which are seen, but at the things which are not seen. For the things which are seen are temporary, but the things which are not seen are eternal. (2 Corinthians 4:16-18)

Momentary Light Affliction

Let's have a look at some of the things that Paul called "light affliction." Because we are not familiar with the terminology of some of the things that happened to Paul, we just read right over it, not realizing what actually happened. Apostle Paul definitely had a revelation of "by His stripes you were healed." Here is a further description of his "light affliction."

From the Jews five times I received forty stripes minus one. Three times I was beaten with rods;

233

once I was stoned; three times I was shipwrecked; a night and a day I have been in the deep; in journeys often, in perils of waters, in perils of robbers, in perils of my own countrymen, in perils of the Gentiles, in perils in the city, in perils in the wilderness, in perils in the sea, in perils among false brethren; in weariness and toil, in sleeplessness often, in hunger and thirst, in fastings often, in cold and nakedness— besides the other things, what comes upon me daily: my deep concern for all the churches. (2 Corinthians 11:24-28)

I never really understood what some of these things actually entailed until I heard Rick Renner[1], a Greek scholar and student of biblical history, explain some of these punishments, and tortures. Rick has been a missionary in Russia and the former Soviet Union for many years, but has also written several great Christian books. I'll never forget hearing Rick describe, when he taught in our church, the true understanding of being beaten with rods, receiving forty stripes minus one, and being stoned. We just read that Paul had all three of these things happen to him more than once.

So, what does it mean to be beaten with rods? This just sounded to me like being caned, maybe with a bamboo rod, which might leave marks on one's back. No, I learned from Rick Renner's teaching that this was a very specific Roman torture designed to stop a person who was spreading a

---

[1] Rick Renner Ministries, www.renner.org

message of insurrection throughout the Roman Empire from doing so any longer. The description was as follows:

The victim had his feet bound together and then was held tightly by a captor. Another man then took a solid metal bat, (similar to a baseball bat) and began to beat the victim's feet. His goal was to crush every bone in both feet from the ankle down, thereby assuring that the victim would never walk again. This was the method of stopping the message of the victim from spreading any further around the Empire.

We just read Paul's account that this happened to him three times. Normally a person is only beaten with rods one time, since all the bones in his feet are crushed and he is crippled for the rest of his life. The obvious point is that apparently Paul had bicycle knowledge of "by His stripes you are healed," which allowed him to appropriate that covenant promise and be healed each time. Let's look at one instance of this.

Then the multitude rose up together against them; and the magistrates tore off their clothes <u>*and commanded them to be beaten with rods.*</u> *And when they had laid many stripes on them, they threw them into prison, commanding the jailer to keep them securely.*

But at midnight <u>*Paul and Silas were praying and singing hymns to God*</u>*, and the prisoners were listening to them. Suddenly there was a great earthquake, so that the foundations of the prison were shaken; and immediately all the doors were opened and everyone's chains were loosed.* (Acts 16:22-2; 25-26)

We see here that Paul and Silas, after having been beaten with rods, were in the prison praying and singing. They were not crying out, "Oh, God, how could You let this happen to us? Where were You, God?" Paul understood that this was the work of the enemy, not of God, and also that it really didn't matter since he would be healed by the power released through the blood covenant he had with Yeshua. Paul definitely saw life as an ambassador, not a tourist, and from presupposition #4, not #1. He understood exactly why this happened to him. It was a part of the war in which he was engaged. Of course, after the earthquake, he led the Philippian jailer into covenant with Yeshua, and later walked on to Thessalonica.

Without understanding the meaning of being beaten with rods, when you read that after a couple days he walked on to the next city, you may think, "Yeah, so what?" After understanding what just happened to Paul, you think, "Wow! That's amazing. Most people would be crippled for life. But Paul just carried on as if nothing had happened." "By His stripes you are healed!"

In verse 25 of 1 Corinthians 11, we read that Paul five times received forty stripes minus one. Again, I never understood what this meant. I discovered that it did not mean literally 39 lashes. Forty lashes was considered the number that would kill a man. So forty minus one meant one lash less than that which would kill the victim. Paul received this torture five different times. Let me quote below Rick Renner's description of this torture as it pertains to Paul.

"Five Times Received I Forty Stripes Save One[2]

In Second Corinthians 11:24, Paul goes on to say, '*Of the Jews five times received I forty stripes save one.*' This was a Jewish method of punishment, applied to Paul on five different occasions. Deuteronomy 25:2,3 refers to this method when it specifies how the wicked man should be punished: '*And it shall be, if the wicked man be worthy to be beaten, that the judge shall cause him to lie down, and to be beaten before his face, according to his fault, by a certain number. Forty stripes he may give him, and not exceed.*'

This was one of the most vicious treatments of the ancient world. The tortured person's clothing was completely removed so he appeared before his persecutors naked. His arms were tied so he could not defend himself. Then the torturer would begin to lash the prisoner's bare body with a whip made of three long cords, one from calf hide and the other two from donkey hide.

Pieces of glass, bone, and metal were often attached to the end of the cords to make the lashing more memorable. The torturer would hit so hard that the pieces of glass, bone, and metal would lodge into the victim's skin. Then as the cords were jerked backward for the next lash of the whip, those pieces of glass, bone, and metal would rip out significant amounts of flesh. This left horrid scars on the victim's body—permanently.

The first third of these lashes were given across the prisoner's upper chest and face, while the remaining two-thirds of lashes were applied to his back, buttocks, and legs;

---

[2] Renner, Rick. *Sparkling Gems From the Greek.* as posted on Zadds web blog, October 20, 2006.
www.imageofgod.zaadz.com/blog/2006/10/jesus_has_overcome_everything

meanwhile, the victim was forced to bend over to make it easier for the torturer to hit his body. Blood flew everywhere as the cords whipped wildly through the air, making snapping noises as they struck the victim again and again.

But let's think a little deeper. If the whip was made of three cords and Paul received thirty-nine lashes each time, this means he received 117 lashes at each beating! And he went through this grueling exercise on five different occasions, which means 585 lashes were laid across Paul's upper chest, face, back, buttocks, and legs. There wasn't a place on his body that hadn't been beaten or had pieces of flesh ripped out of it!

Paul was so committed to fulfilling his God-given call that he wouldn't let anything stop him! After being repeatedly beaten in this terrible manner, he'd get up, put his clothes back on, and go right back to what he was doing before he was beaten. He had already made up his mind. He would not stop until his mission was complete!

Being beaten was an unpleasant experience. It was definitely a part of the journey that no one would relish. But Paul refused to let this experience become a permanent roadblock to his ministry. He pushed the opposition out of the way, got up, and went on. He overcame in the power of Jesus' name and in the power of the Holy Spirit!"

Again, it is amazing to think that Apostle Paul endured this experience five times and still refers to it as "momentary light affliction." To truly understand the experiential heart revelation (bicycle knowledge) that Paul had of his New Covenant promise of physical healing, let's look at the incident of being stoned. In order to understand what happened in this instance, it is critical to recognize that the purpose of stoning was to kill the victim. Stoning was not over until the person being stoned was dead.

I am told that the ancient practice of stoning by the Jews of Paul's day was as follows. The person to be stoned was thrown into a pit. Then those who were to cast the stones found large stones and tossed them into the pit at the victim. The target was the head. Stoning was not to be concluded until one could see the skull split open and the brains oozing out. At this point, one could be certain that the person being stoned was dead. With this understanding, let's now read the account of Paul's stoning.

Then Jews from Antioch and Iconium came there; and having persuaded the multitudes, they stoned Paul and dragged him out of the city, supposing him to be dead. However, when the disciples gathered around him, he rose up and went into the city. And the next day he departed with Barnabas to Derbe. (Acts 14:19-20)

This is amazing to read. One day Paul is stoned and left for dead. (I'm sure he actually was dead.) However, this does not really present a great problem because the disciples just gather around him and he is raised up. Then the next morning he gets up and walks to Derbe as if nothing has happened. I don't know whether he had a headache or what! This man was definitely not a stranger to the covenants of promise and had a profound revelation of his ambassadorship and the provisions of his covenant available to him.

However, we also observe that Paul did not always know immediately what was needed in order to overcome the strategies of the enemy. Satan and the kingdom of darkness are always looking for areas of our lives which grant them entrance to afflict and destroy us. Unfortunately, the areas of our hearts that have not yet been submitted to the Lordship of Messiah are usually hidden to us. Sometimes others can see these areas, but we cannot. Most frequently there are areas of life in which we are exalting self, trusting in self, and

239

defending and protecting self, and unfortunately are blind to the fact that we are doing so in that area of life. When the enemy discovers these areas, he is able to exploit the deception in our lives and perpetrate his schemes against us through these blind areas. For more insight on this topic, see my book, *Deceived, Who Me?*[3]

What About Paul's Thorn?

I have discovered in my own life that many times the ways in which trust in self has operated in the past will continue to operate in the same manner when I find myself in crisis or under pressure. In other words, when I am walking in the flesh instead of in the spirit, my flesh does not work in some new unusual way. It usually works in about the same way it has in the past. Under pressure, I find that I will tend to revert to the same flesh patterns that have plagued me in the past. I believe that this same thing was true for Apostle Paul. Let's look at the potential areas in which he might have trusted in himself and his own abilities. Below is Paul's description of his life before he entered into covenant with Messiah Yeshua.

...though I also might have confidence in the flesh. If anyone else thinks he may have confidence in the flesh, I more so: circumcised the eighth day, of the stock of Israel, of the tribe of Benjamin, a Hebrew of the Hebrews; concerning

---

[3] Hill, Craig. *Deceived, Who Me?* Littleton, Family Foundations International, 1986

the law, a Pharisee; concerning zeal, persecuting the church; concerning the righteousness which is in the law, blameless. But what things were gain to me, these I have counted loss for Christ. (Philippians 3:4-7)

From this description, it seems evident that the potential open door to the enemy in Paul's life could be pride. I would guess that pride and trust in his own accomplishments might be his greatest potential weakness. A person who was not intelligent and had not accomplished much would probably not struggle with these areas of trust in self. However, even after his conversion, Paul again had incredible revelation and experience with God. Paul had phenomenal accomplishments in his ministry, and as we just saw, experienced and participated in many, many supernatural miracles in his own life and ministry. So I believe that there could certainly have been a subtle potential to trust in his revelations and personal accomplishments. From this perspective, let's now have a look at Apostle Paul's battle with what he terms "a thorn in the flesh."

For though I might desire to boast, I will not be a fool; for I will speak the truth. But I refrain, lest anyone should think of me above what he sees me to be or hears from me. And lest I should be exalted above measure by the abundance of the revelations, a thorn in the flesh was given to me, a messenger of Satan to buffet me, lest I be exalted above measure. Concerning this thing I pleaded with the Lord three times that it might depart from me. And He said to me, "My grace is sufficient for you, for My strength is made perfect

241

in weakness." Therefore most gladly I will rather boast in my infirmities, that the power of Christ may rest upon me. Therefore I take pleasure in infirmities, in reproaches, in needs, in persecutions, in distresses, for Christ's sake. For when I am weak, then I am strong. (2 Corinthians 12:6-10)

I would like to look at this passage from a little different perspective than you may have seen it before. This passage has frequently been taught from the perspective of presupposition #1 that God is in control. From this perspective, God is responsible for the event, and the event is not evil, but rather is just. This understanding then goes on to teach the following: God didn't want Paul to be exalted. So God sent a messenger of Satan to torment Paul. When Paul asked God three times to remove this messenger of Satan, God refused to do so. God then told Paul that His grace would be available and sufficient for Paul to continue on retaining and accepting the presence of the messenger of Satan in his life. Paul responded then by saying that he was happy to retain the messenger of Satan in his life because it constantly reminded him of his need to trust in Messiah and not in himself.

I would like at this point to offer another frame of reference regarding this passage by viewing it from the perspective of presupposition #4. From this perspective, God is not responsible for the event, and the event is evil and not just. Let's first look at the players involved in this drama. I think that there are commonly some wrong assumptions made about who is doing what. The players involved are Paul, God, Satan, and a messenger of Satan. So who exactly is doing what?

Paul tells us firstly that he had some incredible revelations. Then he said that there was a potential problem of him being exalted above measure. The first question is: Which person is the subject of the verb *to exalt*: Paul, Satan or God? Who wanted to exalt Paul? Some English translations of this passage translate the verb "exalt" as a reflexive verb, "to exalt myself." However, I am told that this verb, to exalt, is not reflexive in the Greek text. So in English the translation should not be "to keep me from exalting myself," but rather, "to keep me from being exalted," or as is correctly translated in the King James and New King James versions, "lest I be exalted."

The original text then lets us know that it is not Paul who is seeking to exalt himself. He is not the subject of the verb "to exalt," but rather is the object. This leaves Satan and God to do the exalting. Would Satan want to exalt Paul? Did Satan want to make Paul a higher profile person? I think the

> God desired Paul to humble himself that God might exalt him.

answer probably is, no. Satan wanted to diminish Paul, not to exalt him. This leaves us with God as the subject of the verb to exalt. I believe that it was God's purpose to greatly exalt Paul.

Therefore humble yourselves under the mighty hand of God, that He may exalt you in due time. (1 Peter 5:6)

God desired Paul to humble himself that God might exalt him. I have many times heard people say that God uses circumstances to humble us. However, I find in scripture that most of the time God does not humble people, but rather as in the passage above, He calls people to humble themselves. So Satan's plan is to humiliate us, while God's plan is for us to humble ourselves so that He might exalt us.

Was the Thorn From God or From Satan?

Second question: Who gave Paul a thorn in the flesh, defined as a messenger of Satan? This should be fairly easy to solve. Firstly, what does "of Satan" mean? I would think that it means "derived from or emanating from Satan." So who sends messengers of Satan? Would it stand to reason that it would not be God? If it were a messenger sent from God, it probably would have been called, "a messenger of God." So it seems to me that God sends messengers "of God," and Satan sends messengers "of Satan." Therefore, since this was a messenger of Satan, I believe that Satan sent this messenger, and therefore Satan gave Paul the thorn in the flesh. I'm sorry to belabor this point, but I have many times heard people say that God sent Paul the thorn in the flesh, defined as a messenger of Satan. This makes no sense to me.

What was the purpose of the messenger of Satan? It seems that a messenger of Satan would probably naturally work the works of Satan, the devil. If this is true, then what would Yeshua's purpose in Paul's life be regarding the works of this messenger of the devil? Remember 1 John 3:8? *For this purpose the Son of God was manifested, that He might destroy the works of the devil.* So Yeshua, who is the Son of God, came that He might destroy the works of the devil.

Now if God were the One who had sent the thorn in the flesh or messenger of Satan, then we would have the Son of God being manifested that He might destroy the works of the devil, which are actually the works of God. So we would have God and the Son of God opposing each other in purpose. This, of course, makes no sense. I say this only that it might be clear that in truth we have both God and the Son of God purposing together in Paul's life to destroy the works of the devil that were being perpetrated by the messenger of Satan.

So far we are seeing that God gave Paul incredible revelations. God wanted Paul to humble himself so that God could exalt him beyond measure. Satan wanted to limit or measure Paul's exaltation, or if possible even diminish Paul. So Satan sent Paul a thorn in the flesh, which Paul called a messenger of Satan to "buffet" him, lest he be exalted. Buffet is the Greek word *kolaphizo* (Strong's number 2852[4]), which literally means to beat with the fists, maltreat, or treat with violence.

Another question: Who gave this messenger access to be able to buffet Paul? I believe that Paul did. It was Paul's pride and trust in self, in his revelations, and in his ministry that created an open door for Satan to send his messenger into Paul's life. This is why God wanted Paul to humble himself, which would have shut the door to this enemy. Paul had authority to open the door through pride, and Paul had authority to close this door through humility.

However, it seems that Paul initially didn't remember that God had delegated authority over Satan and all of his messengers on earth to man. So Paul began to cry out to the LORD to remove the messenger. The problem was that the LORD was not the one who had sent the messenger. So Paul

---

[4] Strong, James. *The Exhaustive Concordance of the Bible.* New York : Abingdon Press,.1890.

was asking God to do something that He had delegated authority to Paul to do. Paul's pride and trust in his own strength granted this enemy legal authority to buffet Paul. However, he was initially deceived and unaware of this. I have found that crying out to God to remove that which I have granted legal access to never works. Paul discovered this in crying out three times to God about removing this messenger of Satan.

Grace Sufficient for Bondage or Freedom?

God then instructed Paul in saying, *"My grace is sufficient for you, for My strength is made perfect in weakness."* Let's look at the meaning of this sentence. Is God saying, "My grace is sufficient to allow you to remain in your pride and self-trust, and to retain you in bondage to the messenger of Satan who is afflicting you?" NO, of course not.

What is grace? Years ago I ran across a definition of grace that is so much more than the usual "unmerited favor." I would like to share it with you here. Grace is "God's empowering presence exerting a divine influence upon your heart, resulting in manifest change in your life."

The word "sufficient" used here is the Greek work *arkeo*, (Strong's number 714[5]). Some of the Strong's Concordance definitions of this word are:

"Apparently a primary word [but probably akin to 142 through the idea of raising a barrier]

---

[5] *ibid.*

1) to be possessed of unfailing strength

1a) to be strong, to suffice, to be enough

1a1) to defend, ward off"

Hopefully you can see that God is not telling Paul that he is supposed to just accept the presence of a messenger of Satan in his life. God is not telling Paul that His grace is sufficient to remain in bondage to this messenger of Satan, but rather that His grace already extended to Paul by blood covenant is sufficient to "raise up a banner, or barrier, to defend and ward off this messenger of Satan." If you look at several other places that this word is used in scripture, it is never used to say that something is sufficient to retain the problem. No, what is given is sufficient to eliminate the problem.

For example, this word is used regarding food in John 6:7. Yeshua asked his disciples to buy food for the multitude. Philip then told Yeshua that even two hundred denarii (a large sum of money) worth of bread would not be sufficient for the crowd. What does sufficient mean? Sufficient to retain them in hunger, or sufficient to eliminate the hunger? To eliminate the hunger, of course!

God then tells Paul that His (dunamis) power is made perfect in Paul's weakness. Let's look at this word "weakness." It is the Greek word "asthenia," (Strong's number 769[6]). It means, "impotence, weakness, feebleness," or Vines Bible Dictionary[7] gives us the definition, "inability

---

[6] *ibid.*

[7] Vine, W.E., Unger, Merrill F., & White, William, Jr. *An Expository Dictionary of Biblical Words,*. New York:, Thomas Nelson Publishers. 1984. p. 1216

to produce results." I believe that this last definition "inability to produce results" really best describes the meaning of this word. So God is telling Paul here, "My supernatural dunamis power is made manifest through your human inability to produce results."

So using these definitions, I would translate this statement that God spoke to Paul like this: "**My empowering presence exerting a divine influence upon your heart resulting in manifest change in your life is sufficient or avails to raise up a barrier, to ward off, and to remove from you the Satanic messenger and loose you; for My supernatural, miraculous power is consummated and made manifest through your feebleness and inability to produce results in and of yourself.**"

> "My supernatural dunamis power is made manifest through your human inability to produce results."

I believe that with this revelation, Paul quit begging God regarding the messenger of Satan. Instead he let God's grace expose his pride and self-trust and then repented. This repentance then terminated the open door of his flesh's operation, giving the enemy legal access to retain a messenger of Satan in his life. He then was able to exercise the authority granted to him by covenant with God and eliminate the messenger of Satan.

With this revelation and freedom, Paul then states that he would gladly boast in his inability to produce results, because this is what releases the supernatural power of Messiah to deliver from bondage. Paul further states: "*Therefore I take pleasure in infirmities* (weakness–asthenia in Greek), *in reproaches, in needs, in persecutions, in distresses, for Christ's sake. For when I am weak, then I am strong.*" The reason that he is taking pleasure in his "asthenia" rather than in his revelations and ministry is because it is through retaining himself in the position of humility and trust in Messiah's supernatural power that he is then powerful in accomplishment. God's power is released through Paul's authority when he is free from the diminishing influences of Satan that afflict him through trusting in his own revelations and ability to produce results.

Thus I believe that this passage takes us on a journey of Paul's progressive revelation. He starts with a trust in himself in pride. This opens a door in the flesh for Satan to afflict him and keep God from exalting him. He cries out to God, asking God to do what God has already given Paul authority by covenant to do. However, Paul can't exercise his authority because he still has the door open to the enemy through his pride and trust in his own abilities. Finally, he gets the revelation from the LORD that he is trusting in himself instead of in God's grace, which releases God's power for deliverance. Therefore in the future, Paul will no longer boast in his revelations and in his own abilities, but rather in his personal inability to produce results, which allows him to operate in delegated ambassadorial authority to release the covenant power of God for deliverance and to accomplish Kingdom purpose.

Let's then review the two different ways that this passage could be viewed depending on whether one sees life from presupposition #1 or #4. From the vantage point of presupposition #1, we would say that Paul was in danger of exalting himself in pride. God did not want this to happen. God is in control and is like a puppet master who has Satan and his entire kingdom in His hand as puppets. God's purpose is to humble Paul and purge him of his pride. So God sends a messenger of Satan to afflict (buffet) Paul. When

Paul asks the LORD three times to remove this messenger of Satan, God refuses and tells Paul that He will extend His grace to him so that Paul would be able to endure the presence of the messenger of Satan. So Paul finally accepts the fact that he will just have to live being tormented by a messenger of Satan that God sent into his life to make sure that he remains humble. This messenger of Satan then is a constant reminder to Paul that he is weak and that God is the strong one.

From the vantage point of presupposition #4, we would see this entirely differently. Here God wants to exalt Paul, and Satan wants to debase and destroy Paul. Satan is not controlled by God, but rather is an enemy of God's doing everything he can to destroy the purpose of God in Paul's life. Yeshua came to destroy the works of the devil, not to author them or even permit them in Paul's life. Satan has no authority to afflict Paul, except the authority Paul voluntarily or unknowingly gives him. The primary means by which Satan and the kingdom of darkness is given entrance in one's life is through sin, iniquity, or lack of understanding of delegated covenantal authority. So Satan is searching for such a hidden area in Paul's life. If he can find one, He then has legal authority to afflict Paul in this area.

The hidden areas in Paul's life that Satan seems to find are Paul's pride, trust in himself, and trust in his revelations. Satan then accesses these areas and sends his messenger to afflict (buffet) Paul in hopes of debasing, discouraging, and destroying him. Paul, in his pain and ignorance, then appeals to God three times to rid him of this messenger of Satan. However, God let's Paul know that He didn't send the messenger, but rather that the messenger is "of Satan." Consequently, God doesn't have authority over a messenger of Satan, because that authority has been delegated by the New Covenant to Paul.

Paul, however, at this point is a stranger to the covenants of promise, is acting as a private citizen or tourist, and is begging God to do what God has already done. God isn't going to do again what He has already released in covenant by the blood of Messiah Yeshua. Authority over Satan and every demonic messenger has already been released to us by Covenant. So God lets Paul know that His grace has already been made available by the blood of Yeshua in covenant, and that this grace is sufficient to release God's supernatural power to deal with and eliminate any messenger of Satan. However, this authority and power could not be released if Paul remained strong in his own pride as a tourist, but could only be released if Paul became weak in himself and as an ambassador, accessed the covenant authority and power "in Messiah."

Paul then realizes the open door of pride and trust in self. He repents of his pride and self-trust, and accesses the power of God available by His grace to rid him of the messenger of Satan. Paul then tells us that he now realizes that God's power is released and manifested when he humbles himself. He becomes weak in self, but strong as an ambassador and covenant representative of God's, thus releasing God's power to deal with Satan and his messenger.

In the end, Paul tells us that troubles, persecutions, reproaches, and even the frustration of his own inability to produce results are no longer a problem to him. Rather these are just part of the warfare on the planet, and are actually great indicators of areas in his own life that grant entrance to the enemy and need to be brought to death. Paul says that he actually now takes pleasure in these things because every time one of them hits his life, it identifies another open door to the enemy. He then has opportunity to bring that area of sin or iniquity to death in Messiah, so that resurrection life and power might flow back to and through him.

Reflection

1. Suffering, adversity, and injustice are guaranteed by scripture to be a part of your life.

2. Apostle Paul considered serious beatings and even stoning as "momentary light affliction."

3. Paul's thorn can be viewed from at least two different perspectives.

4. How have you responded to suffering and adversity in your life?

5. When you have been under pressure and afflicted, how have you learned how to access God's grace in order to manifest and perfect His power through your weakness?

Resources

📖 *Deceived, Who Me?*

chapter 11
WHAT ABOUT JOB?

J ust as we saw Paul's struggle in the last chapter between
a trust in his own revelation and achievements,
throughout all of human history, man has always had a
struggle between relating to God on the basis of his works or
on the basis of God's covenant word. God, however, has
always related to man on the basis of covenant. As we saw in
Paul's life, begging God as a tourist to change a circumstance
rarely accomplishes anything other than frustration for the
one begging.

Tension Between Works and Covenant

In any situation, the issue is always, "what did God say,"
as opposed to "what am I going to do" or "God, please do
something." Starting way back in the very early chapters of
Genesis when man first sinned, the conflict between man's
religious works and God's blood covenant promise came into
tension. After Adam and Eve sinned, they immediately
recognized their exposed nakedness, and quickly made a
covering out of fig leaves in an attempt to hide from God.
When they then encountered God, He removed the covering
made from human effort, shed the blood of animals and

covered Adam and Eve with the bloody skins of the slain animals. God thus began to teach man from the beginning that blood must always be shed in covenant to atone for sin.

Throughout the history if Israel we see a tension between Covenant word and human works. For Israel the question has been: Do we relate to God on the basis of our keeping the Law (works) or on the basis of blood sacrifice offered in the temple (covenant). This tension has persisted in the hearts of men and women even to this day.

Several years ago, a wonderful, gifted, godly pastor in our city died of cancer at an early age. I remember several times hearing Christians say, "I wonder why God let him die. He was such a godly, selfless, giving pastor." Here we see the false belief in people's hearts that God somehow relates to believers on the basis of their "selfless giving and good works," rather than on the basis of His covenant word. There may be many natural, physiological, nutritional, genetic, emotional, and spiritual reasons why someone could die. However, one's kind heart and good works are definitely not the basis upon which physical health or healing is released from God. If these qualities were that basis, then no kind, giving, selfless people would ever die. We observe that this is simply not the case. In truth, healing is released by faith in the blood covenant promise of Messiah Yeshua (Jesus Christ), not by anyone's revelation, character, selfless giving or good works.

Over the years I have noticed that like Apostle Paul, the longer we walk in relationship with the Lord, the more subtle is the temptation to trust in our own revelations, works, and in the things we have to offer God. When we first entered into covenant relationship with God, most of us realized that we had nothing to offer Him. We were just grateful that Yeshua had given His life to forgive our sin and to open the door to covenant with the Father. However, as time goes on we have a tendency to begin to think that we really do have something to offer God and that He is really pretty fortunate to have us in His Kingdom. Let me give you a simple example.

Suppose Tom, a disciple, becomes sick with the flu. However, Tom hears that there is a guest speaker with a powerful ministry of physical healing, speaking and praying for people at his congregational gathering that evening. Even though Tom would really rather stay home in bed, he makes his way to the meeting hoping that God will use the speaker to bring healing to his physical body. Tom sits through the service, his body racking with pain, until finally there is an invitation for people to come forward for prayer. Tom makes his way up to the front where the speaker asks him what the problem is. Tom tells him of his sickness, and the man then prays a powerful, anointed prayer for healing to manifest in Tom's body.

Tom feels nothing and returns back to his seat just as sick as he was when he arrived at the service. He remains a while longer and observes as others are prayed for. One woman goes forward for prayer whom Tom knows to be a very ungodly and immoral woman. She has rarely come to his congregation, but for some reason shows up tonight requesting prayer for a serious sexually transmitted disease. As the speaker prays for her, she is visibly shaken by the power of God and falls to the floor. After lying there for some time, this woman retreats to the ladies room. Upon returning, she makes her way back up to the front and in tears of joy reports to the speaker and then to everyone that God has completely healed her of her disease. The symptoms are totally gone and she could tell that she was healed when the power of God first hit her.

There Tom sits in his chair, still sick as a dog, and this "immoral woman" is completely healed. Something in Tom's heart cries out, "God, that's not fair! That ought not to be. You heal her and You don't heal me. She has a disease that comes as a result of her immoral lifestyle, and she gets healed? Why? Is that what You honor, God, immorality? Lord, I have given my whole life for You. I consistently tithe my money. I pray at least an hour every day, and daily spend significant time in Your Word. I spend most of my time serving others and live a pretty selfless life. This woman doesn't even come regularly to the congregation, never reads the Bible, is not committed to You, and You heal her and not me. Why?"

Perhaps you can already see the subtle deception and pride in Tom's thinking. Without realizing it, when Tom is thinking this way, where is his trust? It is actually in his own righteousness, good works and the thought that he now somehow "deserves" to be healed. And this "immoral woman" does not "deserve" to be healed. So without realizing it, Tom is not trusting in the covenant promise of God for healing on the basis of the shed blood of Messiah Yeshua. Instead, he is trusting in his godly lifestyle and religious works which he believes should qualify him to be healed. The "immoral woman," on the other hand, has no righteousness or works of her own in which to trust. She can only trust in the New Covenant promise of God.

The woman came to the meeting out of desperation, knowing that she deserved nothing but the sickness that was upon her. She realizes that she certainly doesn't "deserve" to receive healing or anything else from God. However, she heard the speaker say that healing was released by God according to His word that He gave when He made the New Covenant by the shed blood of Messiah. He also said that anyone who was willing to give up his or her life and enter into that New Covenant could receive physical healing not based on his or her own behavior or righteousness, but rather based on the behavior and righteousness of Yeshua. This was extremely good news to this woman, since she knew that her own behavior and righteousness would earn her no favor or benefit with God at all.

Since she had nothing of her own to be able to trust in, this woman was willing to exchange her life in covenant for the life of Messiah and put her total trust in His righteousness and in God's covenant promise for healing. In doing so, she was healed. So what was the difference between Tom, who had been a disciple in covenant with God for years, and this "immoral woman?" The difference was that Tom was trusting in self and didn't know it, and the woman had nothing other than the covenant promise of God in which to trust. When this type of deception is operative, as it was in Tom's heart, God is then blamed for not healing him, and the lie in his own heart is further confirmed that God really is a respecter of persons. The truth is that Tom was not trusting in the covenant word of God, but rather in himself, but didn't know it.

The discussion above now leads us into a look at the book of Job. As we look at Job, we will see that exactly this same deception in which Tom operated overcame Job and severely perverted the way in which he perceived God. Job was trusting in himself and his works and didn't know it.

Four Possible Perspectives on Job

Whenever the topic of suffering or injustice comes up, very quickly someone says, "Well, what about Job?" I believe that the book of Job is an incredible study of what happens when covenant is abandoned and one begins to relate to God on the basis of works. As we saw in chapter four, there are always four different perspectives from which we can view any life experience pertaining to God's responsibility and justice. Let's now review these four possible perspectives and apply them to Job's life. They would be as follows:

Presupposition	Is God Responsible?	Is This Just?
1	YES	YES
2	YES	NO
3	NO	YES
4	NO	NO

Let's now summarize in sentence form what each of these positions represent from Job's perspective.

1. God is the author of my affliction, and this affliction is indeed just. The reason it seems unjust is that we don't understand God's thoughts and ways. I don't understand how my circumstance is kind and good, but I do believe that God is kind and good. Therefore I will continue to trust Him.

2. God is the author of my affliction, and this affliction is not just. I don't deserve it. Therefore, God is not just and I am very angry at Him for doing this to me. God is my tormenter and I am trying to figure out how to get Him to stop this or to somehow get away from Him.

3. God is not the author of my affliction. Satan is. However, this is just and I deserve it.

4. God is not the author of my affliction. Satan is. This is not just but rather is consistent with the character and

nature of Satan. God is my only source of help and comfort.

So before we even get started looking into the book of Job, let me give you my summary of how these four presuppositions play out in the life of Job. Again, most believers will tend to see the book of Job through the lens of either position one or four. Most unbelievers will see Job through the lens of position two. Again, not many will see through the lens of position three. As you might suspect, I tend to see the book of Job through the lens of position four.

As we look into the book, we will see that Job first sees life from position one. As the affliction ensues, his mind continues to attempt to see life from position one, but his heart has definitely moved into position two. It is not until chapter forty-two that we finally see Job unite his heart and his mind together in position four. Let's now look into the book of Job.

Who Was Job?

There was a man in the land of Uz, whose name was Job; and that man was blameless and upright, and one who feared God and shunned evil. And seven sons and three daughters were born to him. Also, his possessions were seven thousand sheep, three thousand camels, five hundred yoke of oxen, five hundred female donkeys, and a very large household, so that this man was the greatest of all the people of the East. And his sons would go and feast in their houses, each on his appointed day, and would send and invite their three sisters to eat and drink with them. So it was, when the days of feasting had run their course, that Job would send and sanctify them, and he would rise early in the morning and offer burnt offerings according to the number of them all. For Job said, "It may be that my sons have sinned and cursed God in their hearts." Thus Job did regularly. (Job 1:1-5)

First of all, we know that Job lived during the time of the patriarchs. So this would be around the time of Abraham, Isaac and Jacob. We see here that Job was a very wealthy and very godly man. As a matter of fact, Job was the greatest and wealthiest man in all "the East." He was a sheik, or a king as it were. He had great wealth, wisdom, and authority. However, he was also a very godly man. We will see later that he used his wealth and wisdom not on his own selfish desires, but rather to bless and benefit those around him.

The word "blameless" is used to describe Job. Some have thought that this meant that Job didn't sin. However, this is not the meaning of the word, and we know that there is only one without sin, and His name is Yeshua, not Job (Romans 3:23). Two other men in the Bible were called blameless; Noah and Zechariah. Noah certainly was not without sin, and when Zechariah was told that his wife, Elizabeth, would have a child (John the Baptist), he was filled with so much unbelief that the angel stopped his mouth until the baby was born. So he was definitely not without sin. Blameless actually just means one who has integrity, and walks in the light he has. Job had an awesome reverence for God and did everything he knew to do to avoid evil and obey God.

We know from verse 5 that Job had some sort of covenant with God. Whenever you see a man offering burnt offerings to Yahweh (God), you know that he is doing so according to a covenant that was made between them. We don't have knowledge of the provisions of the covenant, but we do see Job relating to God on the basis of covenant in verse five of chapter one. Unfortunately, we will not find Job relating to God on the basis of covenant again until verse five of chapter forty-two.

When affliction, persecution, or tragedy strikes our lives, we can either respond to God and life circumstances from the covenant foundation of ambassadorship, or from the personal works foundation of a tourist. In review, covenant understands that I am an ambassador with authority, and am in need of knowing the word of my King so I can speak and enforce it against His (and my) enemies. So the issue in covenant is, "What has God said?" I can then act as an ambassador with His authority to enforce what He has said.

> Covenant understands that I am an ambassador with authority, and am in need of knowing the word of my King so I can speak and enforce it against His (and my) enemies.

A tourist relying upon his own works, on the other hand, says, "What have I done to deserve this?" Furthermore, "What am I going to do now?" A tourist then begins begging and pleading with God to change the circumstance. This, of course, has no impact upon the enemy who is a perpetrator of the destruction, and simply continues to destroy. Since God operates by covenant, begging Him to do what He has already given His ambassador authority to do also has no impact upon the circumstance. Thus the tourist ends up in total frustration and never does understand what really happened to him. He feels that he has been treated very unjustly by God, and can't understand why God would allow such a thing to happen to him since he didn't "deserve" it. After verse five of chapter one, we find Job responding pretty much out of this tourist mentality.

As we continue, let's look now at Job's response to the destruction of Satan in his life. We will come back at a later point in this chapter and look at the interaction between Satan and God in Job chapters one and two. No matter how you understand the interaction between Satan and God in the first two chapters, it is critical to understand that it is Satan who is attacking Job, and not God. Job's battle is not with God, but rather with Satan. Job's only hope of deliverance and victory is to run to God, access His covenant word, and enforce it against Satan.

It seems, however, that Job has little to no awareness of Satan and the warfare that is being waged against him at all. He seems to be living only in a two-party paradigm, in which God and man are the only players. This lack of knowledge of who is actually destroying him creates a huge potential for Satan to pervert the image of God in Job's sight. Satan's strategy is to attack and devastate Job, and then to turn around and get Job to unwittingly ascribe to God the destructive works of Satan. This then keeps Job in a place where his heart is totally closed to God. However, he is unaware of the hardened shell around his heart. Rather than understanding that God is continually available to him, he is totally closed to God. Job's experience is that God has left him and is unavailable.

The Balance Scale

In chapters one and two, Satan destroys Job's family, possessions and health. Job, of course, is devastated. However, in his mind, Job is attempting to still see God as kind and loving, even though he has ascribed these works of Satan to God. In chapter six, verses one through four, Job describes how he sees his affliction.

Then Job answered, 'Oh that my vexations were actually weighed, and laid in the balances together with my iniquity. For then it would be heavier than the sand of the seas, Therefore my words have been rash. For the arrows of the Almighty are within me; Their poison my spirit drinks; The terrors of God are arrayed against me.' (Job 6:1-4) NASB

In verse two, we see that Job has set up a balance scale in his mind. On one side he would like to place his iniquity, and on the other side he would like to place his "vexation," or the affliction. Like Tom in the earlier story, we see here that Job is seeing life from the works, rather than the covenant perspective. He believes that he should be treated in life according to his works, or according to what he "deserves." He is convinced that his affliction is far heavier than what his iniquity would warrant. Therefore, he would like to place his iniquity and his affliction on two sides of a balance scale and prove to God and his three counselors that he has been treated unjustly. He can prove that his affliction far outweighs his iniquity. This, of course, is a fallacious theory of reality and has no effect whatsoever on Satan to get the affliction stopped.

As we progress through the various discourses with Job's three counselors, unfortunately we discover that they also believe this works/balance scale theory of life. The summation of multiple chapters of discourse between Job and the three counselors boils down to an argument between them about whether Job deserves the affliction or not. Job's argument goes something like this.

"Brothers, I know my own heart. I am very sensitive to my own sin and iniquity. I realize that I am not perfect and have sinned in some ways, but not in such a way as to deserve this degree of punishment. God has made some sort of terrible mistake, and if I can just get to Him and explain that this is unjust, I'm sure that God, being just, will relent and stop this torment."

The counselors' argument goes something like this. "Job, you are in denial and are fooling yourself. God, by definition, is just. The very fact that this affliction has come upon you is proof that your iniquity is such as to warrant exactly this degree of affliction. You have gotten exactly what you deserve, because God's character demands that it cannot be any way other than totally just. So stop trying to justify yourself and just admit that you have greatly sinned and you do deserve this. Then repent and God will stop the affliction."

Job's response to this goes something like this. "Brothers, I understand what you are saying, but I also know my own heart, and I don't deserve this. I would be happy to repent of what I have done wrong, but I cannot repent of things I have not done. If I could just get to God, I could present my case and I know He would see what a mistake He has made, and make it right. I really don't deserve this."

The problem here, of course, is that God relates and always has related to man by covenant, not by balance scales and works. Unfortunately, both Job and his counselors all believe this balance scale theory of life and spend a lot of time arguing about whether Job deserves this degree of affliction or not. Arguing with God or people about the injustice of a situation does nothing to deter Satan from continuing to destroy. God is not the thief and He, of course, already agrees that everything Satan does is unjust. Evil and injustice is the nature and character of Satan.

Job's Perverted Image of God

As the affliction progresses, unfortunately Job's heart is embracing a very false image of who God really is. Since Job seems to have very little knowledge that Satan is the perpetrator of the destruction in his life, he has ascribed Satan's destruction to God. Since Job sees life from presupposition #1, he is trying to maintain the image in his mind that God is good. However, in his heart, Job has allowed the enemy to establish a very false and perverted image of God. In chapter nine, Job, in his frustration, begins to give us some insight as to how his heart really perceives God. Let' read this passage:

16 If I called and He answered me, I would not believe that He was listening to my voice. 17 For He crushes me with a tempest, And multiplies my wounds without cause. 18 He will not allow me to catch my breath, But fills me with bitterness. 19 If it is a matter of strength, indeed He is strong; And if of justice, who will appoint my day in court? 20 Though I were righteous, my own mouth would condemn me; Though I were blameless, it would prove me perverse. 21 "I am blameless, yet I do not know myself; I despise my life. 22 It is all one thing; Therefore I say, 'He destroys the blameless and the wicked.' 23 If the scourge slays suddenly, He laughs at the plight of

265

the innocent. 24 The earth is given into the hand of the wicked. He covers the faces of its judges. If it is not He, who else could it be? (Job 9:16-24)

We first see here in verse 16 that Job is very frustrated that he can't seem to communicate with God, so much so, that even if God answered him, he would not even believe that it was God. Obviously God doesn't care enough to even answer Job, or so he thinks. In verse 17 we read that God is someone who crushes Job and multiplies his wounds "without cause." God is totally unjust. He doesn't need a cause to hurt you. He is God, so He can just inflict pain arbitrarily for fun. Does that sound like God to you? This is who Job thinks God is at this point. In verse 18 he says that God won't even let him catch his breath. In other words, God just keeps kicking him, even when he's on the ground with the wind knocked out of him. No honorable contender would do so in a "fair fight."

In verse 19 we find that God uses His "superpowers" and position to His advantage. God has supreme strength, so it's not a fair fight regarding strength. And God is the supreme judge, so you can never have your fair day in court, when your opponent is the judge.

In verse 21 Job again affirms that he is "blameless" and thereby not deserving of what God has done to him. God is the unrighteous one. Job is "blameless." In verse 22, Job tells us that there is really no point to even argue, because God is totally arbitrary. He gathers up the innocent along with the guilty, arbitrarily lumps them all together and then destroys them for no reason. There is absolutely no defense in innocence since God is arbitrary and destroys the innocent the same as He does the guilty. Not only that, but as the innocent are being unjustly punished and killed, God then laughs at and mocks the plight of the innocent. So God is not only arbitrary and unjust, He is also cruel and evil.

In summary, here is Job's heart image of God. "God is someone who doesn't care about you, and won't ever answer you. He seeks you out and even though you are innocent, He summarily declares you guilty for no reason. Then He begins to torture you. He knocks you down and just keeps kicking and kicking you, and won't let you get your breath back. Because He is God, He doesn't fight fair. There is no one stronger than He, or a higher judge or court to which you can appeal for justice. As God tortures you along with the truly guilty, He mocks you and laughs at your plight while He slowly tortures you ultimately to death."

Now if you believed this about God in your heart, how much chance is there that you would run toward Him for comfort, help and protection? Absolutely none. You would close your heart to that kind of God and do everything possible to avoid Him. The strange thing is that while Job embraces this false image of position #2 in his heart, in his mind he still holds to position #1 that God is good and just. This is the classic division between heart and mind that we find afflicts so many believers whose intellectual theology embraces the position #1 that "God is in control." However, when adversity strikes their lives, the false image of position #2 becomes deeply rooted in their hearts.

Though He Slay Me...

As we move on to chapter thirteen, we really see the anger and frustration of Job's heart begin to come out. In his pride and frustration, he really begins to become quite sarcastic and mocking toward God. Because Job believes that God rather than Satan is the author of his distress, He is convinced in his heart that God is cruel and unjust. In verses two and three, we see that Job would still like to find God and argue with Him. He is convinced that he can prove to God that God is wrong.

What you know, I also know; I am not inferior to you. But I would speak to the Almighty, and I desire to reason with God. (Job 13:2-3)

Many times we hear part of Job 13:15 quoted as a righteous statement. In the first part of the verse Job states, *"Though He slay me, yet will I serve Him,"* or *"...hope in Him."* I wonder if you have ever heard quoted the second part of the sentence. Most people only know the first part that I quoted above. The second part of the verse is the following: *"Nevertheless, I will argue my ways before Him. This also will be my salvation."*

Whoa! The argument of Job's ways before God will be his salvation? In verse 18 he further states, *"Behold now, I have prepared my case; I know that I will be vindicated."* This is not a righteous statement. This is the epitome of pride and self-righteousness!

Be silent before me so that I may speak; then let come on me what may. Why should I take my flesh in my teeth and put my life in my hands? Though He slay me, I will hope in Him. Nevertheless I will argue my ways before Him. This also will be my salvation, for a godless man may not come before His presence. Listen carefully to my speech, and let my declaration fill your ears. Behold now, I have prepared my case; I know that I will be vindicated. (Job 13:13-18) NASB

A friend of mine once paraphrased this statement as follows: "Though He slay me, yet my pride and self-righteousness reigns." With the image of God in his heart that we just read about in chapter nine, Job is now declaring his own righteous position in contrast to his perception of God's unrighteous and unjust position. In this passage Job is basically saying, "I would like to find God and argue my case with Him. However, He won't even answer me. He is totally unjust, evil and cruel. He has tortured, tormented and mocked me. However, I am righteous and will maintain my integrity and honor of Him. I will not stoop to His level and treat Him the way that He has treated me. As a matter of fact, even if in His injustice and cruelty, He kills me, I will still serve Him. Nevertheless, I will not take my death lying down, but when He shows up to kill me, I will argue my ways before Him. This will be my salvation, because I know that I am right. I have prepared my case, and when I finally have opportunity to present it to God, He will have to listen and admit that I am right, that I don't <u>deserve</u> this, and that He has acted unjustly. Once God hears my case, He will have to admit that He is wrong and He will repent, and I shall be vindicated!"

What an incredible trap the enemy has set for Job. In reality, where is Job's only source of help and defense against Satan? It is in his covenant relationship with God. However, since Job believes that God is in control, Satan has used that theology to convince Job that God is the one destroying him. Satan has then been able to impart into Job's heart the false image of God we read in chapter nine. In response, Job has now hardened his heart against God, and deepened his trust in self in more intense pride and self-righteousness.

Consequently, there is no way that Job can get his heart open to God to even ask the question, "What has God said?"

Thus he has no way to access his covenant with God to be able to act in his authority and enforce God's word against Satan. I have seen so many believers fall into the same trap when adversity hits their lives. This is a great strategy of the enemy to first find a weak area, launch a destructive attack, and then isolate the victim from God by convincing him/her that God, being in control, was the one behind the attack. This leaves the victim devastated, unable to hear from God because of the blame toward Him in the heart and paralyzed at the mercy of the enemy.

Let's look briefly at one more expression of Job's heart regarding God.

Know then that <u>*God has wronged me*</u> *and has closed His net around me. Behold, I cry, 'Violence!' but I get no answer; I shout for help, but there is no justice.* (Job 19:6-7)

Job's Trust Before the Affliction

Remember the little story I told earlier about the immoral woman who was healed, while the long-time believer, Tom, was not. We talked about a subtle deception that plagued Tom, causing him to trust in himself and his own works while he thought he was trusting in Yeshua and His covenant promises. I believe that this same deception is one of the primary doorways through which Satan found easy access to Job's life. In chapter twenty-nine, Job describes his former life before the affliction started. In this passage, he gives us quite a bit of insight into where his trust might have been positioned. He was convinced that he was trusting God. As you read the following passage, you might keep your eyes and ears open to take note of any frequently repeated words.

*Job further continued his discourse, and said:
"Oh, that I were as in months past As in the days
when God watched over me; When His lamp
shone upon my head, And when by His light I
walked through darkness; just as I was in the days
of my prime, when the friendly counsel of God
was over my tent; when the Almighty was yet
with me, when my children were around me;
when my steps were bathed with cream, and the
rock poured out rivers of oil for me! When I went
out to the gate by the city, when I took my seat in
the open square, the young men saw me and hid,
and the aged arose and stood; the princes
refrained from talking, and put their hand on
their mouth; the voice of nobles was hushed, and
their tongue stuck to the roof of their mouth.
When the ear heard, then it blessed me, and when
the eye saw, then it approved me; because I
delivered the poor who cried out, the fatherless
and the one who had no helper. The blessing of a
perishing man came upon me, and I caused the
widow's heart to sing for joy. I put on
righteousness, and it clothed me; my justice was
like a robe and a turban. I was eyes to the
blind, and I was feet to the lame. I was a father
to the poor. And I searched out the case that I did
not know. I broke the fangs of the wicked, and
plucked the victim from his teeth. Then I said, 'I
shall die in my nest, and multiply my days as the
sand. My root is spread out to the waters, and the
dew lies all night on my branch. My glory is fresh*

within me, and my bow is renewed in my hand.'
Men listened to me and waited, and kept silence
for my counsel. After my words they did not
speak again, and my speech settled on them as
dew. They waited for me as for the rain, and they
opened their mouth wide as for the spring rain. If
I mocked at them, they did not believe it, and the
light of my countenance they did not cast down. I
chose the way for them, and sat as chief; so I
dwelt as a king in the army, as one who comforts
mourners. " (Job 29:1-25)

Did you notice any particular words that were repeated over and over again? How about, "I," "my," and "me." I-yai-yai-yai-YAI!

In this passage in which we hear Job describe his life before the affliction, it becomes very obvious that his trust had been placed in his own righteous works. And truthfully, in comparison with others, Job probably was more righteous, godly and selfless than anyone else around. He recounts how he used his wealth and wisdom to help the poor, widows, orphans, and the disenfranchised of the land. *"I was eyes to the blind, feet to the lame. I was a father to the poor,"* he recounts in verses fifteen and sixteen. *"They waited for me as for the rain, and they opened their mouth wide as for the spring rain,"* he says in verse twenty-three. While all of this is wonderful and no doubt very pleasing to God, the subtle deception of the enemy had led Job into pride and to place his trust in his goodness and kind deeds as a basis for favor and protection with God. Without realizing it, Job was actually a stranger to the covenant, and thus was not able to find God's covenant promise to him and enforce it against the enemy when Satan attacked him.

With this type of pride and trust in his own good deeds, Job had a wide open door in his life of invitation to Satan to destroy him, but unfortunately, was totally unaware of it. One other open door to the enemy in Job's life was fear. We read in chapter three, verse twenty-five, *"For the thing I greatly feared has come upon me, and what I dreaded has happened to me."* In my ministry to people, I have found that the three primary doors that grant access to the enemy are fear, pride and rebellion.

Again, the primary issue in dealing with the attacks of Satan and the kingdom of darkness is to act as a covenant ambassador rather than a tourist. Asking the question, "Why? I don't deserve this," is indicative of a "balance scale" mentality. This is a person who is a tourist, a stranger to the covenant, and has inadvertently placed his trust in his own works. The man who understands his ambassadorship and his covenant is not surprised by adversity, persecution, suffering or trouble, as he realizes that he is part of an invading army living in a war zone. His questions are not, "Why? What did I do to deserve this?" or "What am I going to do now?" His question is, "What has God said? and "Father, how do you want me to apply and enforce your covenant word and Kingdom policy against Your enemies in this situation?"

Unfortunately, Job never saw the reality of who God really was and the fact that God was for him and not against him until chapter forty-two. He lived in his fear, pride, anger, resentment and false images of God for nine months of the affliction. I believe that Job could have stopped the affliction in nine minutes, nine days, or nine months depending upon his perception of God and his willingness to enforce God's covenant word against Satan, rather than remaining in the position of being a victim at the mercy of Satan, but all the while in his heart blaming God.

Finally in Job 42:5-6 we see Job express a revelation he has received of the truth of who God really is. He said,

"I have heard of You by the hearing of the ear, but now my eye sees You. Therefore I abhor myself, and repent in dust and ashes." (Job 42:5-6)

Before this, Job thought he knew God, but in reality had only heard of Him. Now he says he knows Him and has truly seen Him. This vision of the true God elicits the response of repentance of his pride and self-righteousness. We see a totally different attitude manifested in Job in chapter forty-two. Actually in verse seven, we find that God is still very displeased with Job's three counselors because they still hold a false image of God and still believe the fallacious "balance scale" theory of life and relationship with God. We also find in verse eleven that Job's brothers and sisters still believe this too and are still ascribing Satan's attack on Job to God. However, in the end, God the redeemer, restores to Job double that which Satan had destroyed.

Many times we hear people quote another famous statement from Job, thinking it is correct and is truth to be embraced. This statement is: *"The LORD giveth, and the LORD taketh away; Blessed be the name of the LORD."* (Job 1:21) While it is true that Job said this, this statement was certainly not the truth. The truth was, **"The LORD giveth, and Satan taketh away, and the LORD restoreth double; blessed be the name of the LORD."**

274

Satan's False Accusation of God

Let's now return to chapters one and two and have a look at the conversation between God and Satan. Many people believe that God had a special hedge of protection around Job which He then took down at Satan's bidding. It seems that God may have set some sovereign limits on Satan regarding Job, but I believe that Satan had access to Job even before the conversations in chapters one and two.

Now there was a day when the sons of God came to present themselves before the LORD, and Satan also came among them. And the LORD said to Satan, "From where do you come?" So Satan answered the LORD and said, "From going to and fro on the earth, and from walking back and forth on it." Then the LORD said to Satan, "Have you considered My servant Job, that there is none like him on the earth, a blameless and upright man, one who fears God and shuns evil?" So Satan answered the LORD and said, "Does Job fear God for nothing? Have You not made a hedge around him, around his household, and around all that he has on every side? You have blessed the work of his hands, and his possessions have increased in the land. But now, stretch out Your hand and touch all that he has, and he will surely curse You to Your face!" And the LORD said to Satan, "Behold, all that he has is in your power; only do not lay a hand on his person." So Satan went out from the presence of the LORD. (Job 1:6-12)

In verse six, God asks Satan, *"Have you considered my servant Job?"*

It is traditionally taught that God on purpose pointed Job out to Satan and basically said to Satan regarding Job, "Sick 'em." However, I don't believe that this is how the conversation went. God was not pointing Job out to Satan, but rather Satan had already been observing Job, and had an accusation against God as being a respecter of persons. God knew this and drew this accusation out of Satan in the conversation.

When God questioned Satan, obviously He was not seeking information. He is God and knew exactly where Satan had been and what he had been doing. This was a rhetorical question. So a paraphrase of the conversation might be, "Where have you been Satan? What have you been doing? Did you focus your attention on my servant Job, the blameless and upright man?"

Satan then responded, "As a matter of fact, I did focus on Job. And God, the reason I singled him out is that I think You are a respecter of persons. Job is your favorite. You bless him exceedingly and You have a special hedge of protection around him and his household. But Job only loves and blesses You because You have blessed him and protected him."

The fact that God has a special hedge of protection around Job is Satan's false accusation against God. It is not the truth. Many people, however, have also believed Satan's false accusation against God. Because it is written in the Bible, people think that this is truth. While it is true that Satan said this, it is not true that God had a special hedge of protection around Job. God is not a respecter of persons. This is Satan's false accusation against God.

In verse twelve, God then responds to Satan by telling him, "All that he has is in your power" (literally "in your hand"). I don't believe that in this statement God took down a special hedge. There was no special hedge. The only protection that anyone on the planet has ever had against Satan is the covenant word that has been given by God. We have a much better covenant today by the blood of Messiah Yeshua than the one Job had, but nonetheless, Job had some covenant word from God. God does not have favorites today either. The same opportunity to be grafted into the New Covenant is available to everyone and the same covenant promises are available to be received and enforced by everyone. God does not have a special protection around anyone.

When God said in verse twelve, "All he has is in your hand," he was simply restating a fact. Since Adam and Eve gave away their authority over the earth to Satan, the entire earth and all mankind came under the dominion and authority of Satan (1 John 5:19). The only degree to which this was not so was any covenant God made with men that granted them access to His sovereign authority.

In order to understand this phrase, let's look at another place in scripture in which this same phrase is used. We find Abram using this same Hebrew phrase in Genesis sixteen. This phrase was spoken by Abram to Sarai regarding her maid, Hagar. This occurred shortly after Hagar had birthed Ishmael, and Sarai was now unhappy with Abram because Hagar had a son by Abram, and Sarai had none. She was complaining that she was now despised in the sight of her own maid, Hagar, and that this was somehow the fault of her husband, Abram. She wanted Abram to do something about it.

Then Sarai said to Abram, "My wrong be upon you! I gave my maid into your embrace; and when she saw that she had conceived, I became despised in her eyes. The LORD judge between you and me." So Abram said to Sarai, "<u>Indeed your maid is in your hand</u>; do to her as you please." And when Sarai dealt harshly with her, she fled from her presence. (Genesis 16:5-6)

When Abram said to Sarai, "Indeed, your maid is in your hand," was he taking down a special hedge of protection that he had established around Hagar? Was he now releasing a new authority over Hagar to Sarai that she hadn't had before? NO! He was simply reminding her, "Don't blame me for anything pertaining to Hagar. She is your maid. The authority over her life is already in your hand. Do with her as you will."

In Job 1:12, and 2:6, God is saying a similar thing to Satan. "Don't accuse Me of having a special hedge around Job. All that he has is already in your hand. I have given him a covenant and to the extent that he trusts Me and enforces my covenant word against you, you won't be able to touch him. To the extent that he is trusting in himself and his own defenses, you will be able to access his life. However, you do not have authority to kill him." With this, Satan went out from the presence of God and simply operated in the authority that Adam and Eve had given him on the earth to work destruction in the life of Job.

I believe that the most critical thing regarding the book of Job is to see it from a covenant perspective. Without understanding that Job had a covenant with God, and that his only source of deliverance and power to combat the true enemy was in the covenant word of God, it is not possible to see what Job could have done differently. Since Job confused the players in the battle and ascribed to God the works of Satan, he spent all his time arguing with God and with people, rather than asking these simple questions: "God what have You said?" "Who is Your enemy and consequently my enemy?" "How do I enforce Your covenant word against Your enemy?" Even if you believe that God did have a special hedge of protection around Job that was taken down, it is still critical to understand that Satan was the one who attacked Job. God was still in actuality Job's only source of help and deliverance.

Job was totally confused as to the identity of his attacker, and his covenant source of help. Consequently, Job blamed God and allowed the adversity to establish an extremely perverted picture of God in his heart. This false image further kept Job from being able to get his heart open to experience God and find out the truth of who God was, and who the true enemy was. In believing that "God was in control," Job simply fell victim to his circumstances, arguing with God and his counselors that he didn't "deserve" such adversity.

Many people today unfortunately have fallen into this subtle deception as Job did, of trusting in their own works and righteousness without knowing that they have done so. When adversity hits their lives, they then, like Job, blame God in their hearts. In doing so, they fall into the same type of fatalistic paralysis, literally not knowing what to do, while continuing to be devastated by the enemy.

The only way out of this is to begin to tear down the stronghold belief that "God is in control," and break the power of the victim paradigm. Then you can begin to relate to God on the basis of covenant and ask the questions, "What has God said?" and "How am I to enforce His covenant word as His ambassador?" As you move out of the role of a tourist and into the role of an ambassador, you will begin to relate to adversity and to the enemy from an entirely new perspective. This then opens the door for you to partner with God in combining His power and wisdom with your delegated authority to accomplish His Kingdom purposes.

Reflection

1. There has always been a tension between relating to God on the basis of His covenant promises or on the basis of man's righteous works.

2. The book of Job will be viewed very differently through each of the four stated presuppositions.

3. Job ascribed to God the works of Satan.

4. Job viewed life through the paradigm of a balance scale, rather than through covenant.

5. Through his affliction, Job allowed his image of God to become very distorted and perverted.

6. Before the affliction began, without realizing it, Job's trust lay entirely in himself and his righteous deeds. This pride gave entrance to the enemy in his life.

7. In reality, God is Job's only source of help and comfort. God is not Job's tormentor and enemy, as he thinks.

8. At what times in your life have you blamed God for the works of Satan?

9. In what ways have you allowed the enemy to distort your image of God, making it difficult to get your heart open to God?

Resources

🎧 *The Secret of Job's Patience*

CONCLUSION

In conclusion, the theme running through this entire book is that God created you for the purpose of enjoying relationship with Him. All of life is meant to be a partnership between God and you. Consequently, Satan's primary aim is to destroy your relationship with God and motivate you to live a life independent of the LORD.

Motivating man to make decisions independent of God was Satan's initial tactic even in the original garden. Either Adam or Eve could have instantly put an end to Satan's deception through pursuit of relationship with God. However, they chose not to do so. Let's read the account of the interaction between the serpent and the woman:

Now the serpent was more cunning than any beast of the field, which the LORD God had made. And he said to the woman, "Has God indeed said, 'You shall not eat of every tree of the garden'?" ...Then the serpent said to the woman, "You will not surely die. For God knows that in the day you eat of it your eyes will be opened, and you will be like God, knowing good and evil." (Genesis 3:1; 4-5)

At this point, all Adam needed to do was to say to Eve, "I don't actually remember exactly what God said. I don't know if this serpent is correct or not. Let's go check with God and find out what He really did say, and what He says now. Let's ask Him what He wants us to do as His ambassadors regarding this serpent. We don't make any independent decisions without first checking with our King."

However, neither Eve nor Adam chose to act as ambassadors and to pursue relationship with God. They did not ask God what He had said and then enforce that word against the enemy. Had they done so, the course of human history would have turned out very differently. Satan and his agents still use the same tactics today to gain access to our lives through our pride, rebellion and independence.

Six Ineffective Responses to Adversity

When adversity comes to our lives, many of us respond as tourists rather than ambassadors. As Adam and Eve or Job did, we immediately forget our covenant with God. Rather than asking Him what He said and how He would like us to respond as His ambassadors in the circumstance, we begin questioning God, asking "why?" and looking for someone to blame.

I have found six ineffective responses to adversity frequently pursued by tourists and one correct response pursued by ambassadors. These six responses are predicated upon whom the tourist chooses to blame for the adversity, and whether the response is active or passive. If I have believed that "God is in control," then it is very easy for me to blame God for allowing the adversity. Even if I blame myself, behind this I may still blame God (if He is in control) for not changing me, no matter how hard I have tried. In addition, if I have blamed others, I may also still blame God (if He is in control) for allowing the others to harm me or to create the adversity in my life. Here are the six ineffective responses:

1. Blame God and actively strive through my own arguments or righteous works and performance to appease Him so that He will remove the adversity.

2. Blame God and passively give up in anger and/or self-pity and resign myself to my adversity as a powerless victim of the whims of God.

3. Blame myself and actively strive to change myself through increased will power and self-effort, hoping that by so doing I can remove the adversity.

4. Blame myself and passively give up in disappointment and/or self-pity, and resign myself to my adversity as a powerless victim of my own sin and inadequacies.

5. Blame others and actively let my heart be filled with bitterness, resentment and desire to see those responsible pay for what they have done to me.

6. Blame others and passively give up in self-pity, resigning myself to my adversity as a powerless victim at the mercy of the decisions of others.

One Effective Response to Adversity

Hopefully you can see that none of these responses will draw you into relationship with the LORD. Each of the above responses keeps you independent and isolated from the LORD. Only one response will draw you into relationship with God. That response is not to blame anyone or act as a private citizen or a tourist at all. It is rather to come to God as His covenant partner and ambassador, and through relationship with Him discover what He has said and what He wants to do through you in your present circumstance. The following five steps will help you implement an effective response to adversity.

1. Run into relationship with God, your blood covenant partner.

2. Recognize that while sovereign, God is not in control and is not the one afflicting or destroying you. He rather is your blood covenant partner, and as such is your only source of help, comfort, deliverance, and victory.

   Seeing then that we have a great High Priest who has passed through the heavens, Jesus the Son of God, let us hold fast our confession. For we do not have a High Priest who cannot sympathize with our weaknesses, but was in all points tempted as we are, yet without sin. Let us therefore come boldly to the throne of grace that we may obtain mercy and find grace to help in time of need. (Hebrews 4:14-16)

3. Ask the Holy Spirit to give you revelation of your own fear, pride, rebellion, independence or other doorways that may be giving the enemy access into your life and circumstances.

4. Confess and repent of what He shows you and allow Him to bring truth, healing, freedom, and restoration of soul to your life.

5. Approach God, your King as an ambassador, seeking in relationship with him to discover what His covenant word to you is. Ask the question, "What Has

God said?" not "Why did this happen?" or "What am I going to do?" Once you have God's covenant word, then enforce that word and Kingdom policy against the enemy.

The more you persistently practice these above five steps when adversity comes to your life, the more you will receive true revelation (bicycle knowledge) of God's covenant promises to you and of your role as His Kingdom ambassador within your sphere of influence. In doing so, each time you encounter adversity, a deeper experience of God's word and covenant faithfulness becomes a part of you, producing an ever-increasing transformation of character and manifestation of His Kingdom in your life.

APPENDIX

ABOUT THE AUTHOR

Craig Hill and his wife, Jan, live near Denver, Colorado, U.S.A. Craig and Jan give senior leadership to Family Foundations International (FFI). FFI is a non-profit Christian ministry through which life-changing seminars are conducted in many nations of the world. Craig has written several books, including his best seller, *The Ancient Paths*.

Through his past experience in business, missions, counseling and pastoral ministry, God has given Craig unique insight into marriage, family, financial and in-terpersonal relationships. This has resulted in his ability to identify for many people, root causes of relational conflict, compulsive habits, low self-esteem, workaholism, lack of financial provision and other undesirable life patterns, which are repeated from one generation to the next.

By interweaving personal stories with biblical truths, God has anointed Craig to pierce through the veil of the mind to minister to the depths of the heart, resulting in authentic life change for many.

SEMINARS & COURSES

www.familyfoundations.com

Family Foundations International

Embracing God's Ancient Paths of Blessing–
An Experience of the Heart You'll Never Forget!

Family Foundations (FFI) is a non-profit Christian ministry, based out of Colorado, USA. FFI provides seminars and other tools through local churches and businesses in many countries around the world. Craig & Jan Hill are the founders of FFI.

The Ancient Paths Seminars give solid biblical principles, and Craig Hill's moving examples open the heart for participants to receive truth and rest for their souls. The intent of the teaching is not just for information, but to touch the heart. This often exposes hidden areas of woundedness that have occurred in the participant's life. The small group times allow participants to seek and receive God's powerful truth and light in these areas.

For a schedule of seminars or to locate the FFI office nearest you, please visit www.familyfoundations.com. Seminars are available through FFI Seminar Coordinators. Courses are available for purchase.

SEMINARS

An Ancient Paths Seminar: EMPOWERING RELATIONSHIPS

Empowering Relationships is a teaching and small group seminar highlighting life's relationships with God, self and others. This 12-hour seminar includes the following topics:

- Relational versus Topical Communication
- Winning the Battle Over Destructive Attitudes, Habits and Behavior
- Removing Roots That Damage or Destroy Relationships
- Understanding and Breaking Eight Negative Adult Life Patterns

An Ancient Paths Seminar: BLESSING GENERATIONS

Blessing Generations is a teaching and small group seminar on the power of blessing in seven critical times in life. In this 12-hour seminar, participants learn and experience the power of the blessing as the single most important factor that empowers people to prosper. Come, learn and apply the blessing in your life. Topics include

- Seven Critical Times of Blessing in Our Lives
- Consequences of the Lack of Blessing
- Impartation of the Father's Blessing
- The Power Behind Your Name

THE ANCIENT PATHS SEMINAR

The Ancient Paths Seminar is the original 16-hour seminar including the topics of both Empowering Relationships and Blessing Generations Seminars in a condensed format.

290

An Ancient Paths Seminar: COVENANT MARRIAGE (Covenant Marriage Retreat)

Married couples come to understand God's heart for their marriage, the true meaning of covenant and the power of a covenant commitment!

Learn how to add intimacy and unity as a couple and how to divorce-proof your marriage. The weekend ends in a covenant vows renewal ceremony where many couples realize for the first time the power of the covenant words in the vows they speak, sealing their marriage for life. Topics include:

- Communication in Marriage
- How to Divorce-Proof Your Marriage
- Understanding God's Heart, His Perfect Way, for Your Marriage
- Why the Biblical View On Blood Covenant and the Threshold Covenant Are Critical To Your Marriage
- How Marriage and Covenant Reflect the Image of God

An Ancient Paths Seminar: OVERCOMING ANGER

Overcoming Anger is a seminar that presents practical, biblically-based reasons for anger and solutions to overcome anger and other compulsive habits in people's lives. Topics include:

- The Anger Cycle
- Why Do I Do What I Don't Want To Do?
- Identifying the Real Source of Anger and Frustration

- Removing the Power of People and Circumstances to Control My Life
- Three Key Steps to Overcoming Anger

An Ancient Paths Seminar: TRANSFORMING HEARTS

This is a follow-up (level 2) seminar, which may be attended following any seminar with small group ministry. Topics include:

- The authority of the believer
- Freedom from shame
- Softening the hardened heart
- Refocus on who I am in Christ

An Ancient Paths Seminar: FINANCIAL FOUNDATIONS

This seminar (and its predecessor named "Financial Success" is different from many Christian finance seminars. The teaching does not feature merely "practical" information on finances, but follows Craig Hill's anointed understanding of God's Word in teaching finances from a biblical and heart perspective (Matt. 6:21). Topics include:

- Discover the difference between wealth, riches and money
- What is "Mammon?"
- Learn a systemized guide to getting out of debt
- Learn five scriptural uses of money
- Learn how to release God's blessing in finances

An Ancient Paths Seminar: THE QUESTION

This is an exciting and life-changing teaching and audio/video presentation designed especially for young men and young women, but found to open hearts of men and women of all ages. The Question (a 12-hour event) includes thought provoking teaching on video and small groups where the participants can share, and receive prayer and Holy Spirit-led ministry to the heart. There are two separate versions of The Question, one for women and one for men. The question is, "WHO AM I?" Topics include:

- Who Have I Allowed to Answer That Question For Me?
- What Difference do My Actions Today Make?
- How Should I Relate to the Opposite Gender?
- How Will I Know When I Meet The Right Person Who Is My Future Spouse?

Training for Ministry

FFI's Training is an intensive time of teaching leaders and potential leaders how to identify problems and allow the Holy Spirit to guide in effective prayer ministry through small groups. Prerequisite: You must have completed at least one Family Foundations seminar. Topics include:

- Authority and Leadership
- Philosophy of Ministry
- Process of Ministry
- Ministering to Shame
- Steps of Blessing
- Identifying Strongholds

COURSES

COMMUNICATION IN MARRIAGE: *Renewing the Bond of Love*

This eight-week course, which can be purchased and conducted at the local level, is intended for a small group of married couples with a leader couple. Topics include:

- Why women criticize/accuse, and men don't listen/care
- Why have we lost the feeling of romantic love and how can we regain it?
- Learn to identify and meet the five top priority desires of your spouse
- Emotional cycles and key differences in how men and women cope with stress
- Three steps necessary to solve arguments and resolve conflict
- Conquering the single greatest hindrance to fulfillment in marriage

COURTSHIP: *God's Ancient Path to Romance and Marriage*

Courtship is a 10-week video-based study in courtship versus dating for parents and teens. This material, which can be purchased and conducted at the local level, is designed for a small group (4-5 families) of parents and young people to join together to learn and work through the topic of courtship. The goal of the course is for parents and children to have a thorough understanding of the dangerous implications of dating (the world's system) in order to come into agreement about partnering for the identification of God's choice for the son/daughter's spouse. Topics include:

- God's Plan for Romance
- Courtship vs. Dating
- Standards for Relationships
- The Door to a Young Person's Heart
- Root Causes of Teenage Rebellion
- Eight character qualities to look for in a potential spouse
- Seven Phases of a Godly Courtship

For a full listing of available resources and courses
and a current schedule of seminars, please visit us at
WWW.FAMILYFOUNDATIONS.COM